Git

A Fast and Easy Guide to Version Control

Christian Leornardo

Table of Contents

Git Tutorial

This Book provides basic and advanced concepts of Git and GitHub. Our Git tutorial is designed for beginners and professionals.

Git is a modern and widely used distributed version control system in the world. It is developed to manage projects with high speed and efficiency. The version control system allows us to monitor and work together with our team members at the same workspace.

This tutorial will help you to understand the distributed version control system Git via the command line as well as with GitHub. The examples in this tutorial are performed on Windows, but we can also perform same operations on other operating systems like Linux (Ubuntu) and MacOS.

What is Git?

Git is an open source distributed version control system. It is designed to handle minor to major projects with high speed and efficiency. It is developed to co-ordinate the work among the developers. The version control allows us to track and work together with our team members at the same workspace.

Git is foundation of many services like GitHub and GitLab, but we can use Git without using any other Git services. Git can be used privately and publicly.

Git was created by Linus Torvalds in 2005 to develop Linux Kernel. It is also used as an important distributed version-control tool for the DevOps.

Git is easy to learn, and has fast performance. It is superior to other SCM tools like Subversion, CVS, Perforce, and ClearCase.

Features of Git

Some remarkable features of Git are as follows:

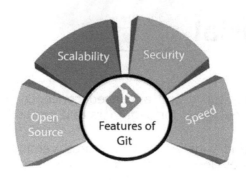

- ❖ Open Source

Git is an open-source tool. It is released under the GPL (General Public License) license.

- ❖ Scalable

Git is scalable, which means when the number of users increases, the Git can easily handle such situations.

- ❖ Distributed

One of Git's great features is that it is distributed. Distributed means that instead of switching the project to another machine, we can create a "clone" of the entire repository. Also, instead of just having one central repository that you send changes to, every user has their own repository that contains the entire commit history of the project. We do not need to connect to the remote repository; the change is just stored on our local repository. If necessary, we can push these changes to a remote repository.

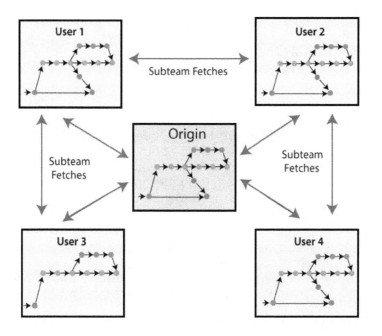

❖ Security

Git is secure. It uses the SHA1 (Secure Hash Function) to name and identify objects within its repository. Files and commits are checked and retrieved by its checksum at the time of checkout. It stores its history in such a way that the ID of particular commits depends upon the complete development history leading up to that commit. Once it is published, one cannot make changes to its old version.

Speed

Git is very fast, so it can complete all the tasks in a while. Most of the git operations are done on the local repository, so it provides a huge speed. Also, a centralized version control system continually communicates with a server somewhere. Performance tests conducted by Mozilla showed that it was extremely fast compared to other VCSs. Fetching version history from a locally stored repository is much faster than fetching it from the remote server. The core part of Git is written in C, which ignores runtime overheads associated with other high-level languages. Git was developed to work on the Linux kernel; therefore, it is capable enough to handle large repositories effectively. From the beginning, speed and performance have been Git's primary goals.

❖ Supports non-linear development

Git supports seamless branching and merging, which helps in visualizing and navigating a non-linear development. A branch in Git represents a single commit. We can construct the full branch structure with the help of its parental commit.

❖ Branching and Merging

Branching and merging are the great features of Git, which makes it different from the other SCM tools. Git allows the creation of multiple branches without affecting each other. We can perform tasks like creation, deletion, and merging on branches, and these tasks take a few seconds only. Below are some features that can be achieved by branching:

> ❖ We can create a separate branch for a new module of the project, commit and delete it whenever we want.
> ❖ We can have a production branch, which always has what goes into production and can be merged for testing in the test branch.
> ❖ We can create a demo branch for the experiment and check if it is working. We can also remove it if needed.
>
> ❖ The core benefit of branching is if we want to push something to a remote repository, we do not have to push all of our branches. We can select a few of our branches, or all of them together.

Data Assurance
The Git data model ensures the cryptographic integrity of every unit of our project. It provides a unique commit ID to every commit through a SHA algorithm. We can retrieve and update the commit by commit ID. Most of the centralized version control systems do not provide such integrity by default.

❖ Staging Area

The Staging area is also a unique functionality of Git. It can be considered as a preview of our next commit, moreover, an intermediate area where commits can be formatted and reviewed before completion. When you make a commit, Git takes changes that are in the staging area and make them as a new commit. We are allowed to add and remove changes from the staging area. The staging area can be considered as a place where Git stores the changes.
Although, Git doesn't have a dedicated staging directory where it

can store some objects representing file changes (blobs). Instead of this, it uses a file called index.

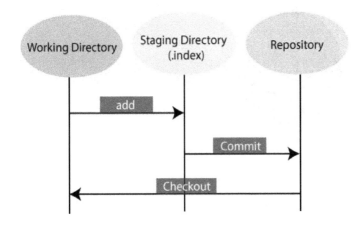

Another feature of Git that makes it apart from other SCM tools is that it is possible to quickly stage some of our files and commit them without committing other modified files in our working directory.

❖ Maintain the clean history

Git facilitates with Git Rebase; It is one of the most helpful features of Git. It fetches the latest commits from the master branch and puts our code on top of that. Thus, it maintains a clean history of the project.

Benefits of Git

A version control application allows us to keep track of all the changes that we make in the files of our project. Every time we make changes in files of an existing project, we can push those changes to a repository. Other developers are allowed to pull your changes from the repository and continue to work with the updates that you added to the project files.

Some significant benefits of using Git are as follows:

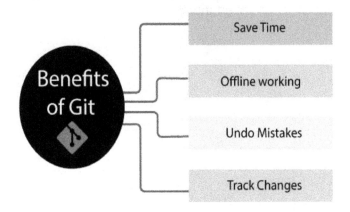

* ❖ Saves Time

Git is lightning fast technology. Each command takes only a few seconds to execute so we can save a lot of time as compared to login to a GitHub account and find out its features.

* ❖ Offline Working

One of the most important benefits of Git is that it supports offline working. If we are facing internet connectivity issues, it will not affect our work. In Git, we can do almost everything locally. Comparatively, other CVS like SVN is limited and prefer the connection with the central repository.

* ❖ Undo Mistakes

One additional benefit of Git is we can Undo mistakes. Sometimes the undo can be a savior option for us. Git provides the undo option for almost everything.

* ❖ Track the Changes

Git facilitates with some exciting features such as Diff, Log, and Status, which allows us to track changes so we can check the status, compare our files or branches.

Why Git?

We have discussed many features and benefits of Git that demonstrate the undoubtedly Git as the leading version control system. Now, we will discuss some other points about why should we choose Git.

❖ Git Integrity

Git is developed to ensure the security and integrity of content being version controlled. It uses checksum during transit or tampering with the file system to confirm that information is not lost. Internally it creates a checksum value from the contents of the file and then verifies it when transmitting or storing data.

❖ Trendy Version Control System

Git is the most widely used version control system. It has maximum projects among all the version control systems. Due to its amazing workflow and features, it is a preferred choice of developers.

❖ Everything is Local

Almost All operations of Git can be performed locally; this is a significant reason for the use of Git. We will not have to ensure internet connectivity.

❖ Collaborate to Public Projects

There are many public projects available on the GitHub. We can collaborate on those projects and show our creativity to the world. Many developers are collaborating on public projects. The collaboration allows us to stand with experienced developers and learn a lot from them; thus, it takes our programming skills to the next level.

❖ Impress Recruiters

We can impress recruiters by mentioning the Git and GitHub on our resume. Send your GitHub profile link to the HR of the organization you want to join. Show your skills and influence them through your work. It increases the chances of getting hired.

What is GitHub?

GitHub is a Git repository hosting service. GitHub also facilitates with many of its features, such as access control and collaboration. It provides a Web-based graphical interface.

GitHub is an American company. It hosts source code of your project in the form of different programming languages and keeps track of the various changes made by programmers.

It offers both distributed version control and source code management (SCM) functionality of Git. It also facilitates with some collaboration features such as bug tracking, feature requests, task management for every project.

Features of GitHub

GitHub is a place where programmers and designers work together. They collaborate, contribute, and fix bugs together. It hosts plenty of open source projects and codes of various programming languages.

Some of its significant features are as follows.

- ❖ Collaboration
- ❖ Integrated issue and bug tracking
- ❖ Graphical representation of branches
- ❖ Git repositories hosting
- ❖ Project management
- ❖ Team management
- ❖ Code hosting
- ❖ Track and assign tasks
- ❖ Conversations
- ❖ Wikisc

Benefits of GitHub

GitHub can be separated as the Git and the Hub. GitHub service includes access controls as well as collaboration features like task management, repository hosting, and team management.

The key benefits of GitHub are as follows.

- ❖ It is easy to contribute to open source projects via GitHub.
- ❖ It helps to create an excellent document.
- ❖ You can attract recruiter by showing off your work. If you have a profile on GitHub, you will have a higher chance of being recruited.
- ❖ It allows your work to get out there in front of the public.
- ❖ You can track changes in your code across versions.

Git Version Control System

A version control system is a software that tracks changes to a file or set of files over time so that you can recall specific versions later. It also allows you to work together with other programmers.

The version control system is a collection of software tools that help a team to manage changes in a source code. It uses a special kind of database to keep track of every modification to the code.

Developers can compare earlier versions of the code with an older version to fix the mistakes.

Benefits of the Version Control System

The Version Control System is very helpful and beneficial in software development; developing software without using version control is unsafe. It provides backups for uncertainty. Version control systems offer a speedy interface to developers. It also allows software teams to preserve efficiency and agility according to the team scales to include more developers.

Some key benefits of having a version control system are as follows.

- ❖ Complete change history of the file
- ❖ Simultaneously working
- ❖ Branching and merging
- ❖ Traceability

Types of Version Control System

- ❖ Localized version Control System
- ❖ Centralized version control systems
- ❖ Distributed version control systems

Localized Version Control Systems

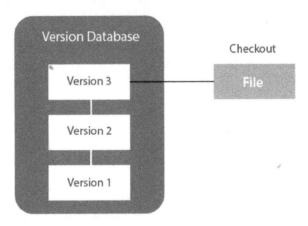

The localized version control method is a common approach because of its simplicity. But this approach leads to a higher chance of error. In this approach, you may forget which directory you're in and accidentally write to the wrong file or copy over files you don't want to.

To deal with this issue, programmers developed local VCSs that had a simple database. Such databases kept all the changes to files under revision control. A local version control system keeps local copies of the files.

The major drawback of Local VCS is that it has a single point of failure.

Centralized Version Control System
The developers needed to collaborate with other developers on other systems. The localized version control system failed in this case. To deal with this problem, Centralized Version Control Systems were developed.

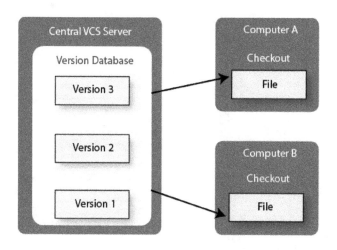

These systems have a single server that contains the versioned files, and some clients to check out files from a central place.

Centralized version control systems have many benefits, especially over local VCSs.

❖ Everyone on the system has information about the work what others are doing on the project.
❖ Administrators have control over other developers.
❖ It is easier to deal with a centralized version control system than a localized version control system.
❖ A local version control system facilitates with a server software component which stores and manages the different versions of the files.

It also has the same drawback as in local version control system that it also has a single point of failure.

Distributed Version Control System

Centralized Version Control System uses a central server to store all the database and team collaboration. But due to single point failure, which means the failure of the central server, developers do not prefer it. Next, the Distributed Version Control System is developed.

In a Distributed Version Control System (such as Git, Mercurial, Bazaar or Darcs), the user has a local copy of a repository. So, the clients don't just check out the latest snapshot of the files even they can fully mirror the repository. The local repository contains all the files and metadata present in the main repository.

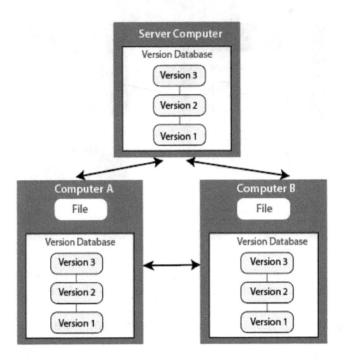

DVCS allows automatic management branching and merging. It speeds up of most operations except pushing and pulling. DVCS enhances the ability to work offline and does not rely on a single location for backups. If any server stops and other systems were collaborating via it, then any of the client repositories could be restored by that server. Every checkout is a full backup of all the data.

These systems do not necessarily depend on a central server to store all the versions of a project file.

Difference between Centralized Version Control System and Distributed Version Control System

Centralized Version Control Systems are systems that use client/server architecture. In a centralized Version Control System, one or more client systems are directly connected to a central server. Contrarily the Distributed Version Control Systems are systems that use peer-to-peer architecture.

There are many benefits and drawbacks of using both the version control systems. Let's have a look at some significant differences between Centralized and Distributed version control system.

Centralized Version Control System	Distributed Version Control System
In CVCS, The repository is placed at one place and delivers information to many clients.	In DVCS, Every user has a local copy of the repository in place of the central repository on the server-side.
It is based on the client-server approach.	It is based on the client-server approach.
It is the most straightforward system based on the concept of the central repository.	It is flexible and has emerged with the concept that everyone has their repository.
In CVCS, the server provides the latest code to all the clients across the globe.	In DVCS, every user can check out the snapshot of the code, and they can fully mirror the central repository.
CVCS is easy to administrate and has additional control over users and access by its server from one place.	DVCS is fast comparing to CVCS as you don't have to interact with the central server for every command.
The popular tools of CVCS are SVN (Subversion) and CVS.	The popular tools of DVCS are Git and Mercurial.
CVCS is easy to understand for beginners.	DVCS has some complex process for beginners.
If the server fails, No system can access data from another system.	if any server fails and other systems were collaborating via it, that server can restore any of the client repositories

Getting Started

How to Install Git on Windows

To use Git, you have to install it on your computer. Even if you have already installed Git, it's probably a good idea to upgrade it to the latest version. You can either install it as a package or via another installer or download it from its official site.

Now the question arises that how to download the Git installer package. Below is the stepwise installation process that helps you to download and install the Git.

How to download Git?

Step1: To download the Git installer, visit the Git's official site and go to download page. The link for the download page is https://git-scm.com/downloads.

Click on the package given on the page as download 2.23.0 for windows. The download will start after selecting the package.

Now, the Git installer package has been downloaded.

Install Git

Step2: Click on the downloaded installer file and select yes to continue. After the selecting yes the installation begins, and the screen will look like as

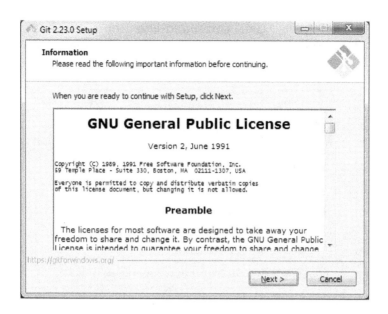

Click on next to continue.

Step3: Default components are automatically selected in this step. You can also choose your required part.

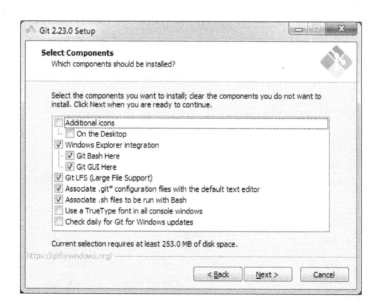

Click next to continue.

Step4: The default Git command-line options are selected automatically. You can choose your preferred choice. Click next to continue.

Step5: The default transport backend options are selected in this step. Click next to continue.

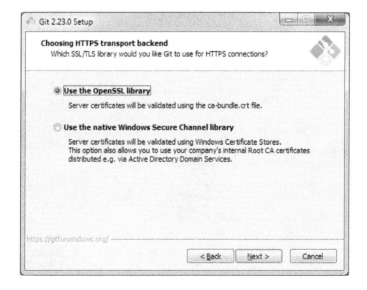

Step6: Select your required line ending option and click next to continue.

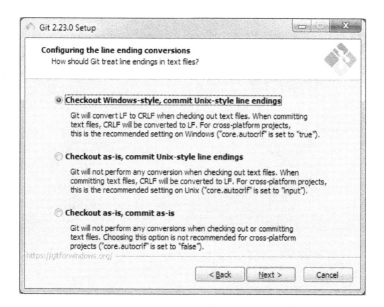

Step7: Select preferred terminal emulator clicks on the next to continue.

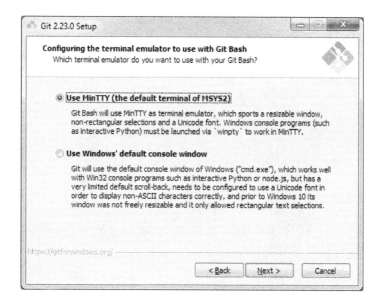

Step8: This is the last step that provides some extra features like system caching, credential management and symbolic link. Select the required features and click on the next option.

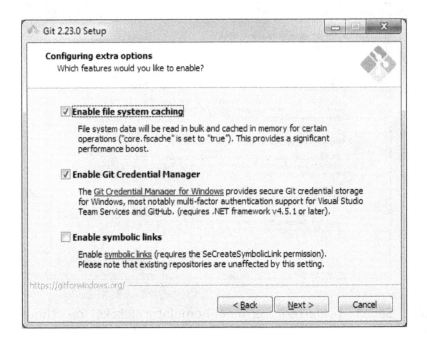

Step9: The files are being extracted in this step.

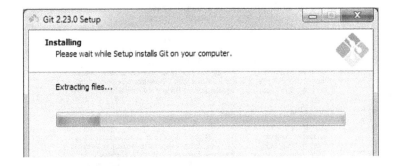

Therefore, The Git installation is completed. Now you can access the Git Gui and Git Bash.

The Git Gui looks like as

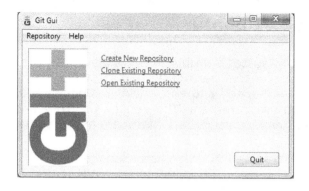

It facilitates with three features.

- ❖ Create New Repository
- ❖ Clone Existing Repository
- ❖ Open Existing Repository

The Git Bash looks like as

Install Git on Ubuntu

Git is an open-source distributed version control system that is available for everyone at zero cost. It is designed to handle minor to major projects with speed and efficiency. It is developed to co-ordinate the work among programmers. The version control allows you to track and work together with your team members at the same workspace.

Git is the most common source code management (SCM) and covers more users than earlier VCS systems like SVN. Let's understand how to install Git on your Ubuntu server.

I have done this installation on Ubuntu 16.04 LTS. But the given commands should also work with the other versions.

Below are the steps to install the Git on Ubuntu server:

Step1: Start the General OS and Package update

First of all, we should start the general OS and package updates. To do so, run the below command:

```
$ apt-get update
```

Now we have started the general OS and package updates. After this, we will run the general updates on the server so that we can get started with installing Git. To do so, run the following commands:

Step2: Install Git

To install Git, run the below command:

```
$ apt-get install git-core
```

The above command will install the Git on your system, but it may ask you to confirm the download and installation.

Step3: Confirm Git the installation

To confirm the installation, press 'y' key on the editor. Now, Git is installed and ready to use.

When the central installation done, first check to ensure the executable file is set up and accessible. The best way to do this is the git version command. It will be run as:

```
$ git --version
```

Output:

```
git version 2.24.0
```

Step4: Configure the Git for the First use

Now you can start using Git on your system. You can explore many features of the version control system. To go with Git, you have to configure the initial user access process. It can be done with the git config command.

Suppose I want to register a user whose user name is "jvtpoint" and email address is "Jvtpoint@xyz", then it will be done as follows:

To register a username, run the below command:

```
$ git config --global user.name "jvtpoint"
```

To register an email address for the given author, run the below command:

```
$ git config --global user.email "jvtpoint@xyz"
```

Now, you have successfully registered a user for the version control system.

It's important to understand that the git config tool works on a user according to the user. For example, if we have a user "john" registered on Git. Then there can be another user "Mike" on the same machine registered on Git. To do this, Mike must run the same command from his user accou nt. The commits made by both the users will be done under their details in Git.

Install Git on Mac

There are multiple ways to install Git on mac. It comes inbuilt with Xcode or its other command-line tools. To start the Git, open terminal and enter the below command:

```
$ git --version
```
The above command will display the installed version of Git.

Output:

```
git version 2.24.0 (Apple Git-66)
```
If you do not have installed it already, then it will ask you to install it.

Apple provides support for Git, but it lags by several major versions. We may install a newer version of Git using one of the following methods:

Git Installer for Mac

This process is the simplest way to download the latest version of Git. Visit the official page of git downloads. Choose the download option for Mac OS X.

The installer file will download to your system. Follow the prompts, choose the required installer option. After the installation process completed, verify the installation was successful by running the below command on the terminal:

```
$ git --version
```
The above command will display the installed version of Git.
Consider the below output.

Output:

```
git version 2.24.0 (Apple Git-66)
```
Now, we have successfully installed the latest version on our mac OS. It's time to configure the version control system for the first use.

To register a username, run the below command:

```
$ git config --global user.name "jvtpoint"
```

To register an email address for the given author, run the below command:

```
$ git config --global user.email "jvtpoint@xyz"
```

Installation via MacPorts

Sometimes MacPorts also referred to DarwinPorts. It makes the straightforward installation of software on the Mac OS and Darwin operating systems. If we have installed MacPorts for managing packages on OS X, follow the below steps to install Git.

Step1: Update MacPorts

To update MacPorts, run the below command:

```
$ sudo port selfupdate
```

Step2: Search for the latest Ports

To search for the most recent available Git ports and variants, run the below command:

```
$ port search git
$ port variants git
```

The above command will search for the latest available port and options and will install it.

Step3: Install Git

To install Git, run the below command:

```
$ sudo port install git
```

We can also install some extra tools with Git. These tools may assist Git in different manners. To Install Git with bash-completion, svn, and the docs, run the below command:

```
$ sudo port install git +svn +doc +bash_completion +gitweb
```

Now, we have successfully installed Git with the help of MacPorts on our system.

Step4: Configure Git

The next step for the first use is git configuration.

We will configure the Git username and email address as same as given above.

To register a username, run the below command:

```
$ git config --global user.name "jvtpoint"
```

To register an email address for the given author, run the below command:

```
$ git config --global user.email "jvtpoint@xyz"
```

Install Git via Homebrew

Homebrew is used to make the software installation straight forward. If we have installed Homebrew for managing packages on OS X, follow the below steps to go with Git:

Step1: install Git

Open the terminal and run the below command to install Git using Homebrew:

```
$ brew install git
```

The above command will install the Git on our machine. The next step is to verify the installation.

Step2: Verify the installation

It is essential to ensure that whether the installation process has been succeeded or not.

To verify whether the installation has been successful or not, run the below command:

```
$ git --version
```

The above command will display the version that has been installed on your system. Consider the below output:

```
git version 2.24.0
```

Step3: Configure Git

We will configure the Git username and email address same as given above.

To register a username, run the below command:

```
$ git config --global user.name "jvtpoint"
```

To register an email address for the given author, run the below command:

```
$ git config --global user.email "jvtpoint@xyz"
```

Git Environment Setup

The environment of any tool consists of elements that support execution with software, hardware, and network configured. It includes operating system settings, hardware configuration, software configuration, test terminals, and other support to perform the operations. It is an essential aspect of any software.

It will help you to understand how to set up Git for first use on various platforms so you can read and write code in no time.

The Git config command

Git supports a command called git config that lets you get and set configuration variables that control all facets of how Git looks and operates. It is used to set Git configuration values on a global or local project level.

Setting user.name and user.email are the necessary configuration options as your name and email will show up in your commit messages.

Setting username

The username is used by the Git for each commit.

```
$ git config --global user.name "Himanshu Dubey"
```

Setting email id

The Git uses this email id for each commit.

```
$ git config --global user.email  "himanshudubey481@gmail.com"
```
There are many other configuration options that the user can set.

Setting editor

You can set the default text editor when Git needs you to type in a message. If you have not selected any of the editors, Git will use your default system's editor.

To select a different text editor, such as Vim,

```
$ git config --global core.editor Vim
```

Checking Your Settings

You can check your configuration settings; you can use the git config --list command to list all the settings that Git can find at that point.

```
$ git config -list
```

This command will list all your settings. See the below command line output.

Output

```
HiMaNshU@HiMaNshU-PC MINGW64 ~/Desktop
$ git config --list
core.symlinks=false
core.autocrlf=true
core.fscache=true
color.diff=auto
color.status=auto
color.branch=auto
color.interactive=true
help.format=html
rebase.autosquash=true
http.sslcainfo=C:/Program Files/Git/mingw64/ssl/certs/ca-
bundle.crt
http.sslbackend=openssl
diff.astextplain.textconv=astextplain
filter.lfs.clean=git-lfs clean -- %f
filter.lfs.smudge=git-lfs smudge --skip -- %f
filter.lfs.process=git-lfs filter-process --skip
filter.lfs.required=true
credential.helper=manager
gui.recentrepo=C:/Git
user.email=dav.himanshudubey481@gmail.com
user.name=Himanshu Dubey
```

Colored output

You can customize your Git output to view a personalized color theme. The git config can be used to set these color themes.

Color.ui

```
$ Git config -global color.ui true
```

The default value of color.ui is set as auto, which will apply colors to the immediate terminal output stream. You can set the color value as true, false, auto, and always.

Git configuration levels

The git config command can accept arguments to specify the configuration level. The following configuration levels are available in the Git config.

- ❖ local
- ❖ global
- ❖ system

--local

It is the default level in Git. Git config will write to a local level if no configuration option is given. Local configuration values are stored in .git/config directory as a file.

--global

The global level configuration is user-specific configuration. User-specific means, it is applied to an individual operating system user. Global configuration values are stored in a user's home directory. ~ /.gitconfig on UNIX systems and C:\Users\\.gitconfig on windows as a file format.

--system

The system-level configuration is applied across an entire system. The entire system means all users on an operating system and all repositories. The system-level configuration file stores in a gitconfig file off the system directory. $(prefix)/etc/gitconfig on UNIX systems and C:\ProgramData\Git\config on Windows.

The order of priority of the Git config is local, global, and system, respectively. It means when looking for a configuration value, Git will start at the local level and bubble up to the system level.

Git Tools

To explore the robust functionality of Git, we need some tools. Git comes with some of its tools like Git Bash, Git GUI to provide the interface between machine and user. It supports inbuilt as well as third-party tools.

Git comes with built-in GUI tools like git bash, git-gui, and gitk for committing and browsing. It also supports several third-party tools for users looking for platform-specific experience.

Git Package Tools

Git provides powerful functionality to explore it. We need many tools such as commands, command line, Git GUI. Let's understand some essential package tools.

GitBash

Git Bash is an application for the Windows environment. It is used as Git command line for windows. Git Bash provides an emulation layer for a Git command-line experience. Bash is an abbreviation of Bourne Again Shell. Git package installer contains Bash, bash utilities, and Git on a Windows operating system.

Bash is a standard default shell on Linux and macOS. A shell is a terminal application which is used to create an interface with an operating system through commands.

By default, Git Windows package contains the Git Bash tool. We can access it by right-click on a folder in Windows Explorer.

Git Bash Commands

Git Bash comes with some additional commands that are stored in the /usr/bin directory of the Git Bash emulation. Git Bash can provide a robust shell experience on Windows. Git Bash comes with some essential shell commands like Ssh, scp, cat, find.

Git Bash also includes the full set of Git core commands like git clone, git commit, git checkout, git push, and more.

Git GUI

Git GUI is a powerful alternative to Git BASH. It offers a graphical version of the Git command line function, as well as comprehensive visual diff tools. We can access it by simply right click on a folder or location in windows explorer. Also, we can access it through the command line by typing below command.

```
$ git gui
```

```
HiMaNshU@HiMaNshU-PC MINGW64 ~/Desktop (master)
$ git gui
```

A pop-up window will open as Git gui tool. The Git GUI's interface looks like as:

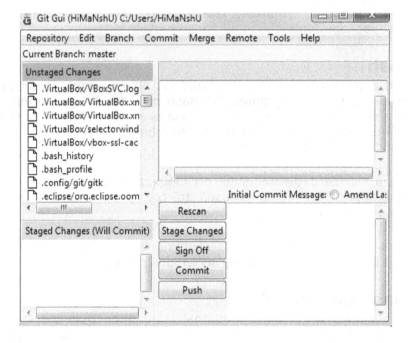

Git facilitates with some built-in GUI tools for committing (git-gui) and browsing (gitk), but there are many third-party tools for users looking for platform-specific experience.

Gitk

gitk is a graphical history viewer tool. It's a robust GUI shell over git log and git grep. This tool is used to find something that happened in the past or visualize your project's history.

Gitk can invoke from the command-line. Just change directory into a Git repository, and type:

```
$ gitk [git log options]
```

```
HiMaNshU@HiMaNshU-PC MINGW64 ~/Desktop (master)
$ cd GitExample2

HiMaNshU@HiMaNshU-PC MINGW64 ~/Desktop/GitExample2 (master)
$ gitk
```

This command invokes the gitk graphical interface and displays the project history. The Gitk interface looks like this:

Gitk supports several command-line options, most of which are passed through to the underlying git log action.

Git Third-Party Tools

Many third-party tools are available in the market to enhance the functionality of Git and provide an improved user interface. These tools are available for distinct platforms like Windows, Mac, Linux, Android, iOS.

Git Terminology

Git is a tool that covered vast terminology and jargon, which can often be difficult for new users, or those who know Git basics but want to become Git masters. So, we need a little explanation of the terminology behind the tools. Let's have a look at the commonly used terms.

Some commonly used terms are:

Branch

A branch is a version of the repository that diverges from the main working project. It is an essential feature available in most modern version control systems. A Git project can have more than one branch. We can perform many operations on Git branch-like rename, list, delete, etc.

Checkout

In Git, the term checkout is used for the act of switching between different versions of a target entity. The git checkout command is used to switch between branches in a repository.

Cherry-Picking

Cherry-picking in Git is meant to apply some commit from one branch into another branch. In case you made a mistake and committed a change into the wrong branch, but do not want to merge the whole branch. You can revert the commit and cherry-pick it on another branch.

Clone

The git clone is a Git command-line utility. It is used to make a copy of the target repository or clone it. If I want a local copy of my repository from GitHub, this tool allows creating a local copy of that repository on your local directory from the repository URL.

Fetch

It is used to fetch branches and tags from one or more other repositories, along with the objects necessary to complete their histories. It updates the remote-tracking branches.

HEAD

HEAD is the representation of the last commit in the current checkout branch. We can think of the head like a current branch. When you switch branches with git checkout, the HEAD revision changes, and points the new branch.

Index

The Git index is a staging area between the working directory and repository. It is used as the index to build up a set of changes that you want to commit together.

Master

Master is a naming convention for Git branch. It's a default branch of Git. After cloning a project from a remote server, the resulting local repository contains only a single local branch. This branch is called a "master" branch. It means that "master" is a repository's "default" branch.

Merge

Merging is a process to put a forked history back together. The git merge command facilitates you to take the data created by git branch and integrate them into a single branch.

Origin

In Git, "origin" is a reference to the remote repository from a project was initially cloned. More precisely, it is used instead of that original repository URL to make referencing much easier.

Pull/Pull Request

The term Pull is used to receive data from GitHub. It fetches and merges changes on the remote server to your working directory. The git pull command is used to make a Git pull.

Pull requests are a process for a developer to notify team members that they have completed a feature. Once their feature branch is ready, the developer files a pull request via their remote server account. Pull request announces all the team members that they need to review the code and merge it into the master branch.

Push

The push term refers to upload local repository content to a remote repository. Pushing is an act of transfer commits from your local repository to a remote repository. Pushing is capable of overwriting changes; caution should be taken when pushing.

Rebase

In Git, the term rebase is referred to as the process of moving or combining a sequence of commits to a new base commit. Rebasing is very beneficial and visualized the process in the environment of a feature branching workflow.

From a content perception, rebasing is a technique of changing the base of your branch from one commit to another.

Remote

In Git, the term remote is concerned with the remote repository. It is a shared repository that all team members use to exchange their changes. A remote repository is stored on a code hosting service like an internal server, GitHub, Subversion and more.

In case of a local repository, a remote typically does not provide a file tree of the project's current state, as an alternative it only consists of the .git versioning data.

Repository

In Git, Repository is like a data structure used by VCS to store metadata for a set of files and directories. It contains the collection of the file as well as the history of changes made to those files. Repositories in Git is considered as your project folder. A repository has all the project-related data. Distinct projects have distinct repositories.

Stashing

Sometimes you want to switch the branches, but you are working on an incomplete part of your current project. You don't want to make a commit of half-done work. Git stashing allows you to do so. The git stash command enables you to switch branch without committing the current branch.

Tag

Tags make a point as a specific point in Git history. It is used to mark a commit stage as important. We can tag a commit for future reference. Primarily, it is used to mark a projects initial point like v1.1. There are two types of tags.

- ❖ Light-weighted tag
- ❖ Annotated tag

Upstream And Downstream

The term upstream and downstream is a reference of the repository. Generally, upstream is where you cloned the repository from (the origin) and downstream is any project that integrates your work with other works. However, these terms are not restricted to Git repositories.

Git Revert

In Git, the term revert is used to revert some commit. To revert a commit, git revert command is used. It is an undo type command. However, it is not a traditional undo alternative.

Git Reset

In Git, the term reset stands for undoing changes. The git reset command is used to reset the changes. The git reset command has three core forms of invocation. These forms are as follows.

- ❖ Soft
- ❖ Mixed
- ❖ Hard

Git Ignore

In Git, the term ignore used to specify intentionally untracked files that Git should ignore. It doesn't affect the Files that already tracked by Git.

Git Diff

Git diff is a command-line utility. It's a multiuse Git command. When it is executed, it runs a diff function on Git data sources. These data sources can be files, branches, commits, and more. It is used to show changes between commits, commit, and working tree, etc.

Git Cheat Sheet

A Git cheat sheet is a summary of Git quick references. It contains basic Git commands with quick installation. A cheat sheet or crib sheet is a brief set of notes used for quick reference. Cheat sheets are so named because the people may use it without no prior knowledge.

Git Flow

GitFlow is a branching model for Git, developed by Vincent Driessen. It is very well organized to collaborate and scale the development team. Git flow is a collection of Git commands. It accomplishes many repository operations with just single commands.

Git Squash

In Git, the term squash is used to squash previous commits into one. Git squash is an excellent technique to group-specific changes before forwarding them to others. You can merge several commits into a single commit with the powerful interactive rebase command.

Git Rm

In Git, the term rm stands for remove. It is used to remove individual files or a collection of files. The key function of git rm is to remove tracked files from the Git index. Additionally, it can be used to remove files from both the working directory and staging index.

Git Fork

A fork is a rough copy of a repository. Forking a repository allows you to freely test and debug with changes without affecting the original project.

Great use of using forks to propose changes for bug fixes. To resolve an issue for a bug that you found, you can:

- ❖ Fork the repository.
- ❖ Make the fix.
- ❖ Forward a pull request to the project owner.

Git command line

There are many different ways to use Git. Git supports many command-line tools and graphical user interfaces. The Git command line is the only place where you can run all the Git commands.

The following set of commands will help you understand how to use Git via the command line.

Basic Git Commands

Here is a list of most essential Git commands that are used daily.

- ❖ Git Config command
- ❖ Git init command
- ❖ Git clone command
- ❖ Git add command
- ❖ Git commit command
- ❖ Git status command
- ❖ Git push Command
- ❖ Git pull command
- ❖ Git Branch Command
- ❖ Git Merge Command
- ❖ Git log command
- ❖ Git remote command

Let's understand each command in detail.

Git config command

This command configures the user. The Git config command is the first and necessary command used on the Git command line. This command sets the author name and email address to be used with your commits. Git config is also used in other scenarios.

Syntax
- ❖ $ git config --global user.name "ImDwivedi1"
- ❖ $ git config --global user.email "Himanshudubey481@gmail.com"

Git Init command

This command is used to create a local repository.

Syntax

```
$ git init Demo
```

The init command will initialize an empty repository. See the below screenshot.

```
HiMaNshU@HiMaNshU-PC MINGW64 ~/Desktop
$ git init Demo
Initialized empty Git repository in C:/Users/HiMaNshU/Desktop/Demo/.git/

HiMaNshU@HiMaNshU-PC MINGW64 ~/Desktop
$ |
```

Git clone command

This command is used to make a copy of a repository from an existing URL. If I want a local copy of my repository from GitHub, this command allows creating a local copy of that repository on your local directory from the repository URL.

Syntax

```
$ git clone URL
```

```
HiMaNshU@HiMaNshU-PC MINGW64 ~/Desktop/Git-example (master)
$ git clone https://github.com/ImDwivedi1/Git-Example.git
Cloning into 'Git-Example'...
remote: Enumerating objects: 3, done.
remote: Counting objects: 100% (3/3), done.
remote: Total 3 (delta 0), reused 0 (delta 0), pack-reused 0
Unpacking objects: 100% (3/3), done.
```

Git add command

This command is used to add one or more files to staging (Index) area.

Syntax

To add one file

```
$ git add Filename
```

To add more than one file

```
$ git add*
```

HiMaNshU@HiMaNshU-PC MINGW64 ~/Desktop/Git-example (master)
$ git add README.md

Git commit command

Commit command is used in two scenarios. They are as follows.

Git commit -m

This command changes the head. It records or snapshots the file permanently in the version history with a message.

Syntax

```
$ git commit -m " Commit Message"
```
Git commit -a

This command commits any files added in the repository with git add and also commits any files you've changed since then.

Syntax

```
$ git commit -a
```

HiMaNshU@HiMaNshU-PC MINGW64 ~/Desktop/Git-example (master)
$ git commit -a -m "Adding the key of c"
[master (root-commit) 758797a] Adding the key of c
 1 file changed, 2 insertions(+)
 create mode 100644 README.md

Git status command

The status command is used to display the state of the working directory and the staging area. It allows you to see which changes have been staged, which haven't, and which files aren?t being tracked by Git. It does not show you any information about the committed project history. For this, you need to use the git log. It also lists the files that you've changed and those you still need to add or commit.

Syntax

```
$ git status
```

```
HiMaNshU@HiMaNshU-PC MINGW64 ~/Desktop/Git-example (master)
$ git status
On branch master
Your branch is based on 'origin/master', but the upstream is gone.
  (use "git branch --unset-upstream" to fixup)

nothing to commit, working tree clean
```

Git push Command

It is used to upload local repository content to a remote repository. Pushing is an act of transfer commits from your local repository to a remote repo. It's the complement to git fetch, but whereas fetching imports commits to local branches on comparatively pushing exports commits to remote branches. Remote branches are configured by using the git remote command. Pushing is capable of overwriting changes, and caution should be taken when pushing.

Git push command can be used as follows.

Git push origin master

This command sends the changes made on the master branch, to your remote repository.

Syntax

```
$ git push [variable name] master
```

```
HiMaNshU@HiMaNshU-PC MINGW64 ~/Desktop/Git-example (mast
er)
$ git push origin master
```

```
HiMaNshU@HiMaNshU-PC MINGW64 ~/Desktop/gitexample2 (master)
$ git push origin master
Everything up-to-date

HiMaNshU@HiMaNshU-PC MINGW64 ~/Desktop/gitexample2 (master)
$
```

Git push -all

This command pushes all the branches to the server repository.

Syntax

```
$ git push --all
```

```
HiMaNshU@HiMaNshU-PC MINGW64 ~/Desktop/gitexample2 (master)
$ git push --all
Everything up-to-date

HiMaNshU@HiMaNshU-PC MINGW64 ~/Desktop/gitexample2 (master)
$
```

Git pull command

Pull command is used to receive data from GitHub. It fetches and merges changes on the remote server to your working directory.

Syntax

```
$ git pull URL
```

```
HiMaNshU@HiMaNshU-PC MINGW64 ~/Desktop/Git-example (master)
$ git pull https://github.com/ImDwivedi1/Git-Example
warning: no common commits
remote: Enumerating objects: 3, done.
remote: Counting objects: 100% (3/3), done.
remote: Total 3 (delta 0), reused 0 (delta 0), pack-reused 0
Unpacking objects: 100% (3/3), done.
From https://github.com/ImDwivedi1/Git-Example
 * branch              HEAD       -> FETCH_HEAD
fatal: refusing to merge unrelated histories

HiMaNshU@HiMaNshU-PC MINGW64 ~/Desktop/Git-example (master)
$
```

Git Branch Command

This command lists all the branches available in the repository.

Syntax

```
$ git branch
```

```
HiMaNshU@HiMaNshU-PC MINGW64 ~/Desktop/gitexample2 (master)
$ git branch
* master

HiMaNshU@HiMaNshU-PC MINGW64 ~/Desktop/gitexample2 (master)
```

Git Merge Command

This command is used to merge the specified branch?s history into the current branch.

Syntax

```
$ git merge BranchName
```

```
HiMaNshU@HiMaNshU-PC MINGW64 ~/Desktop/gitexample2 (master)
$ git merge master
Already up to date.
```

Git log Command

This command is used to check the commit history.

Syntax

```
$ git log
```

```
HiMaNshU@HiMaNshU-PC MINGW64 ~/Desktop/gitexample2 (master)
$ git log
commit 1d2bc037a54eba76e9f25b8e8cf7176273d13af0 (HEAD -> master, origin/master,
origin/HEAD)
Author: ImDwivedi1 <52317024+ImDwivedi1@users.noreply.github.com>
Date:   Fri Aug 30 11:05:06 2019 +0530

    Initial commit
```

By default, if no argument passed, Git log shows the most recent commits first. We can limit the number of log entries displayed by passing a number as an option, such as -3 to show only the last three entries.

```
$ git log -3
```

Git remote Command

Git Remote command is used to connect your local repository to the remote server. This command allows you to create, view, and delete connections to other repositories. These connections are more like bookmarks rather than direct links into other repositories. This command doesn't provide real-time access to repositories.

```
HiMaNshU@HiMaNshU-PC MINGW64 ~/Desktop/gitexample2 (master)
$ git remote add origin https://github.com/ImDwivedi1/GitExample2
fatal: remote origin already exists.
```

Git Flow / Git Branching Model

Git flow is the set of guidelines that developers can follow when using Git. We cannot say these guidelines as rules. These are not the rules; it is a standard for an ideal project. So that a developer would easily understand the things.

It is referred to as Branching Model by the developers and works as a central repository for a project. Developers work and push their work to different branches of the main repository.

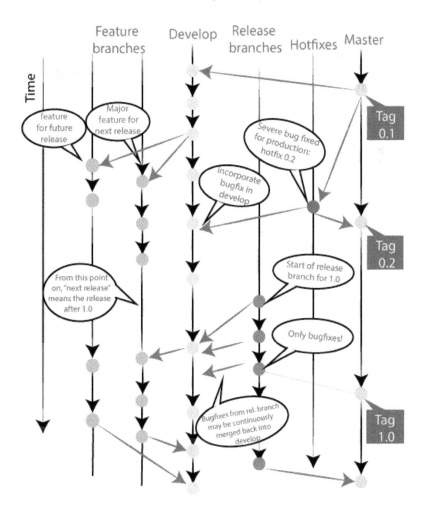

There are different types of branches in a project. According to the standard branching strategy and release management, there can be following types of branches:

- ❖ Master
- ❖ Develop
- ❖ Hotfixes
- ❖ Release branches
- ❖ Feature branches

Every branch has its meaning and standard. Let's understand each branch and its usage.

The Main Branches

Two of the branching model's branches are considered as main branches of the project. These branches are as follows:

- ❖ master
- ❖ develop

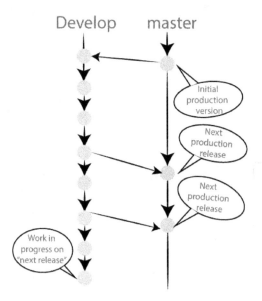

Master Branch

The master branch is the main branch of the project that contains all the history of final changes. Every developer must be used to the master branch. The master branch contains the source code of HEAD that always reflects a final version of the project.

Your local repository has its master branch that always up to date with the master of a remote repository.

It is suggested not to mess with the master. If you edited the master branch of a group project, your changes would affect everyone else, and very quickly, there will be merge conflicts.

Develop Branch

It is parallel to the master branch. It is also considered as the main branch of the project. This branch contains the latest delivered development changes for the next release. It has the final source code for the release. It is also called as a "integration branch."

When the develop branch reaches a stable point and is ready to release, it should be merged with master and tagged with a release version.

Supportive Branches

The development model needs a variety of supporting branches for the parallel development, tracking of features, assist in quick fixing and release, and other problems. These branches have a limited lifetime and are removed after the uses.

The different types of supportive branches, we may use are as follows:

- ❖ Feature branches
- ❖ Release branches
- ❖ Hotfix branches

Each of these branches is made for a specific purpose and have some merge targets. These branches are significant for a technical perspective.

Feature Branches

Feature branches can be considered as topic branches. It is used to develop a new feature for the next version of the project. The existence of this branch is limited; it is deleted after its feature has been merged with develop branch.

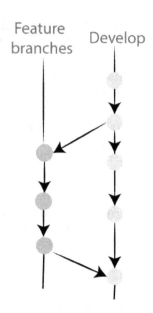

Feature branches   Develop

Release Branches

The release branch is created for the support of a new version release. Senior developers will create a release branch. The release branch will contain the predetermined amount of the feature branch. The release branch should be deployed to a staging server for testing.

Developers are allowed for minor bug fixing and preparing meta-data for a release on this branch. After all these tasks, it can be merged with the develop branch.

When all the targeted features are created, then it can be merged with the develop branch. Some usual standard of the release branch are as follows:

❖ Generally, senior developers will create a release branch.
❖ The release branch will contain the predetermined amount of the feature branch.
❖ The release branch should be deployed to a staging server for testing.
❖ Any bugs that need to be improved must be addressed at the release branch.
❖ The release branch must have to be merged back into developing as well as the master branch.
❖ After merging, the release branch with the develop branch must be tagged with a version number.

Hotfix Branches

Hotfix branches are similar to Release branches; both are created for a new production release.

The hotfix branches arise due to immediate action on the project. In case of a critical bug in a production version, a hotfix branch may branch off in your project. After fixing the bug, this branch can be merged with the master branch with a tag.

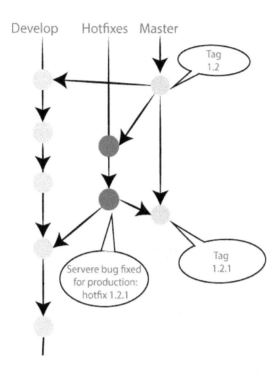

Git Cheat Sheet

1. Git configuration

- Git config
  Get and set configuration variables that control all facets of how Git looks and operates.
  Set the name:
  $ git config --global user.name "User name"
  Set the email:
  $ git config --global user.email "himanshudubey481@gmail.com"
  Set the default editor:
  $ git config --global core.editor Vim
  Check the setting:
  $ git config -list
- Git alias
  Set up an alias for each command:
  $ git config --global alias.co checkout
  $ git config --global alias.br branch
  $ git config --global alias.ci commit
  $ git config --global alias.st status

2. Starting a project

- Git init
  Create a local repository:
  $ git init
- Git clone
  Make a local copy of the server repository.
  $ git clone

3. Local changes

- o Git add
  Add a file to staging (Index) area:
  $ git add Filename
  Add all files of a repo to staging (Index) area:
  $ git add*
- o Git commit
  Record or snapshots the file permanently in the version
  history with a message.
  $ git commit -m " Commit Message"

4. Track changes

- o Git diff
  Track the changes that have not been staged: $ git diff
  Track the changes that have staged but not committed:
  $ git diff --staged
  Track the changes after committing a file:
  $ git diff HEAD
  Track the changes between two commits:
  $ git diff Git Diff Branches:
  $ git diff < branch 2>
- o Git status
  Display the state of the working directory and the staging area.
  $ git status
- o Git show Shows objects:
  $ git show

5. Commit History

- o Git log
  Display the most recent commits and the status of the head:
  $ git log
  Display the output as one commit per line:
  $ git log -oneline

Displays the files that have been modified:
$ git log -stat
Display the modified files with location:
$ git log -p

- ○ Git blame
  Display the modification on each line of a file:
  $ git blame <file name>

6. Ignoring files

- ○ .gitignore
  Specify intentionally untracked files that Git should ignore.
  Create .gitignore:
  $ touch .gitignore List the ignored files:
  $ git ls-files -i --exclude-standard

7. Branching

- ○ Git branch Create branch:
  $ git branch List Branch:
  $ git branch --list Delete a Branch:
  $ git branch -d Delete a remote Branch:
  $ git push origin -delete Rename Branch:
  $ git branch -m
- ○ Git checkout
  Switch between branches in a repository.
  Switch to a particular branch:
  $ git checkout
  Create a new branch and switch to it:
  $ git checkout -b Checkout a Remote branch:
  $ git checkout
- ○ Git stash
  Switch branches without committing the current branch. Stash current work:
  $ git stash

Saving stashes with a message:

$ git stash save ""

Check the stored stashes:

$ git stash list

Re-apply the changes that you just stashed:

$ git stash apply

Track the stashes and their changes:

$ git stash show

Re-apply the previous commits:

$ git stash pop

Delete a most recent stash from the queue:

$ git stash drop

Delete all the available stashes at once:

$ git stash clear

Stash work on a separate branch:

$ git stash branch

o Git cherry pic

Apply the changes introduced by some existing commit:

$ git cherry-pick

8. Merging

o Git merge

Merge the branches:

$ git merge

Merge the specified commit to currently active branch:

$ git merge

o Git rebase

Apply a sequence of commits from distinct branches into a final commit.

$ git rebase

Continue the rebasing process:

$ git rebase -continue Abort the rebasing process:

$ git rebase --skip

- o Git interactive rebase
  Allow various operations like edit, rewrite, reorder, and more on existing commits.
  $ git rebase -i

9. Remote

- o Git remote
  Check the configuration of the remote server:
  $ git remote -v
  Add a remote for the repository:
  $ git remote add Fetch the data from the remote server:
  $ git fetch
  Remove a remote connection from the repository:
  $ git remote rm
  Rename remote server:
  $ git remote rename
  Show additional information about a particular remote:
  $ git remote show
  Change remote:
  $ git remote set-url
- o Git origin master
  Push data to the remote server:
  $ git push origin master Pull data from remote server:
  $ git pull origin master

10. Pushing Updates

- o Git push
  Transfer the commits from your local repository to a remote server. Push data to the remote server:
  $ git push origin master Force push data:
  $ git push -f
  Delete a remote branch by push command:
  $ git push origin -delete edited

11. Pulling updates

- ○ Git pull
  Pull the data from the server:
  $ git pull origin master
  Pull a remote branch:
  $ git pull
- ○ Git fetch
  Download branches and tags from one or more repositories.
  Fetch the remote repository:
  $ git fetch< repository Url> Fetch a specific branch:
  $ git fetch
  Fetch all the branches simultaneously:
  $ git fetch -all
  Synchronize the local repository:
  $ git fetch origin

12. Undo changes

- ○ Git revert
  Undo the changes:
  $ git revert
  Revert a particular commit:
  $ git revert
- ○ Git reset
  Reset the changes:
  $ git reset -hard
  $ git reset -soft:
  $ git reset --mixed

13. Removing files

- ○ Git rm
  Remove the files from the working tree and from the index:
  $ git rm <file Name>
  Remove files from the Git But keep the files in your local

repository:
$ git rm -cached

Staging & Commits

Git Init

The git init command is the first command that you will run on Git. The git init command is used to create a new blank repository. It is used to make an existing project as a Git project. Several Git commands run inside the repository, but init command can be run outside of the repository.

The git init command creates a .git subdirectory in the current working directory. This newly created subdirectory contains all of the necessary metadata. These metadata can be categorized into objects, refs, and temp files. It also initializes a HEAD pointer for the master branch of the repository.

Creating the first repository

Git version control system allows you to share projects among developers. For learning Git, it is essential to understand that how can we create a project on Git. A repository is a directory that contains all the project-related data. There can also be more than one project on a single repository.

We can create a repository for blank and existing projects. Let's understand how to create a repository.

Create a Repository for a Blank (New) Project:

To create a blank repository, open command line on your desired directory and run the init command as follows:

```
$ git init
```

The above command will create an empty .git repository. Suppose we want to make a git repository on our desktop.

To do so, open Git Bash on the desktop and run the above command. Consider the below output:

```
HiMaNshU@HiMaNshU-PC MINGW64 ~/Desktop (master)
$ git init
Initialized empty Git repository in C:/Users/HiMaNshU/Desktop/.git/

HiMaNshU@HiMaNshU-PC MINGW64 ~/Desktop (master)
$
```

The above command will initialize a .git repository on the desktop. Now we can create and add files on this repository for version control.

To create a file, run the cat or touch command as follows:

$ touch <file Name>

To add files to the repository, run the git add command as follows:

$ git add <file name>

Create a Repository for an existing project

If you want to share your project on a version control system and control it with Git, then, browse your project's directory and start the git command line (Git Bash for Windows) here. To initialize a new repository, run the below command:

Syntax:

$ git init

Output:

```
HiMaNshU@HiMaNshU-PC MINGW64 /c/My Project
$ git init
Initialized empty Git repository in C:/My Project/.git/

HiMaNshU@HiMaNshU-PC MINGW64 /c/My Project (master)
$ |
```

The above command will create a new subdirectory named .git that holds all necessary repository files. The .git subdirectory can be understood as a Git repository skeleton. Consider the below image:

.git	10/12/2019 4:04 PM	File folder	
design	9/19/2019 6:10 PM	Cascading Style S...	1 KB
design2	10/6/2019 5:21 PM	Cascading Style S...	1 KB
index	9/19/2019 6:10 PM	JSP File	2 KB
master	9/19/2019 6:10 PM	JSP File	1 KB
merge the branch	9/20/2019 6:05 PM	File	1 KB
newfile	10/4/2019 2:10 PM	Text Document	1 KB
newfile1	10/4/2019 2:10 PM	Text Document	1 KB
newfile2	10/9/2019 12:26 PM	Text Document	0 KB
README	9/19/2019 6:10 PM	MD File	1 KB

An empty repository .git is added to my existing project. If we want to start version-controlling for existing files, we have to track these files with git add command, followed by a commit.

We can list all the untracked files by git status command.

```
$ git status
```

Consider the below output:

```
HiMaNshU@HiMaNshU-PC MINGW64 /c/My Project (master)
$ git status
On branch master

No commits yet

Untracked files:
  (use "git add <file>..." to include in what will be committed)
        README.md
        design.css
        design2.css
        index.jsp
        master.jsp
        merge the branch
        newfile.txt
        newfile1.txt
        newfile2.txt

nothing added to commit but untracked files present (use "git add" to track)
```

In the above output, the list of all untracked files is displayed by the git status command.

We can track all the untracked files by Git Add command.

Create a Repository and Directory Together

The git init command allows us to create a new blank repository and a directory together. The empty repository .git is created under the directory. Suppose I want to create a blank repository with a project name, then we can do so by the git init command. Consider the below command:

```
$ git init NewDirectory
```

The above command will create an empty .git repository under a directory named NewDirectory. Consider the below output:

```
HiMaNshU@HiMaNshU-PC MINGW64 ~/Desktop (master)
$ git init
Initialized empty Git repository in C:/Users/HiMaNshU/Desktop/.git/

HiMaNshU@HiMaNshU-PC MINGW64 ~/Desktop (master)
$ git init NewDirectory
Initialized empty Git repository in C:/Users/HiMaNshU/Desktop/NewDirectory/
.git/
```

In the above output, the directory and the repository both are created.

Hence we can create a repository using git init command. Two other commands are handy to start with git. They are Git Add, and Git commit.

Git Add

The git add command is used to add file contents to the Index (Staging Area).This command updates the current content of the working tree to the staging area. It also prepares the staged content for the next commit. Every time we add or update any file in our project, it is required to forward updates to the staging area.

The git add command is a core part of Git technology. It typically adds one file at a time, but there some options are available that can add more than one file at once.

The "index" contains a snapshot of the working tree data. This snapshot will be forwarded for the next commit.

The git add command can be run many times before making a commit. These all add operations can be put under one commit. The add command adds the files that are specified on command line.

The git add command does not add the .gitignore file by default. In fact, we can ignore the files by this command.

Let's understand how to add files on Git?

Git add files

Git add command is a straight forward command. It adds files to the staging area. We can add single or multiple files at once in the staging area. It will be run as:

```
$ git add <File name>
```

The above command is added to the git staging area, but yet it cannot be shared on the version control system. A commit operation is needed to share it. Let's understand the below scenario.

We have created a file for our newly created repository in NewDirectory. To create a file, use the touch command as follows:

```
$ touch newfile.txt
```

And check the status whether it is untracked or not by git status command as follows:

```
$ git status
```

The above command will display the untracked files from the repository. These files can be added to our repository. As we know we have created a newfile.txt, so to add this file, run the below command:

```
$ git add newfile.txt
```

Consider the below output:

```
HiMaNshU@HiMaNshU-PC MINGW64 ~/Desktop/NewDirectory (master)
$ touch newfile.txt

HiMaNshU@HiMaNshU-PC MINGW64 ~/Desktop/NewDirectory (master)
$ git status
on branch master

No commits yet

Untracked files:
  (use "git add <file>..." to include in what will be committed)
        newfile.txt

nothing added to commit but untracked files present (use "git add" to

HiMaNshU@HiMaNshU-PC MINGW64 ~/Desktop/NewDirectory (master)
$ git add newfile.txt
```

From the above output, we can see newfile.txt has been added to our repository. Now, we have to commit it to share on Git.

Git Add All

We can add more than one files in Git, but we have to run the add command repeatedly. Git facilitates us with a unique option of the add command by which we can add all the available files at once. To add all the files from the repository, run the add command with -A option. We can use '.' Instead of -A option. This command will stage all the files at a time. It will run as follows:

```
$ git add -A
```

Or

```
$ git add .
```

The above command will add all the files available in the repository.
Consider the below scenario:

We can either create four new files, or we can copy it, and then we add all these files at once. Consider the below output:

```
HiMaNshU@HiMaNshU-PC MINGW64 ~/Desktop/NewDirectory (master)
$ git add newfile.txt

HiMaNshU@HiMaNshU-PC MINGW64 ~/Desktop/NewDirectory (master)
$ touch newfile1.txt

HiMaNshU@HiMaNshU-PC MINGW64 ~/Desktop/NewDirectory (master)
$ touch newfile2.txt

HiMaNshU@HiMaNshU-PC MINGW64 ~/Desktop/NewDirectory (master)
$ touch newfile3.txt

HiMaNshU@HiMaNshU-PC MINGW64 ~/Desktop/NewDirectory (master)
$ git status
On branch master

No commits yet

Changes to be committed:
  (use "git rm --cached <file>..." to unstage)
        new file:   newfile.txt

Untracked files:
  (use "git add <file>..." to include in what will be committed)
        newfile1.txt
        newfile2.txt
        newfile3.txt
```

In the above output, all the files are displaying as untracked files by Git. To track all of these files at once, run the below command:

```
$ git add -A
```

The above command will add all the files to the staging area. Remember, the -A option is case sensitive. Consider the below output:

```
HiMaNshU@HiMaNshU-PC MINGW64 ~/Desktop/NewDirectory (master)
$ git add -A

HiMaNshU@HiMaNshU-PC MINGW64 ~/Desktop/NewDirectory (master)
$ git status
On branch master

No commits yet

Changes to be committed:
  (use "git rm --cached <file>..." to unstage)
        new file:   newfile.txt
        new file:   newfile1.txt
        new file:   newfile2.txt
        new file:   newfile3.txt
```

In the above output, all the files have been added. The status of all files is displaying as staged.

Removing Files from the Staging Area

The git add command is also used to remove files from the staging area. If we delete a file from the repository, then it is available to our repository as an untracked file. The add command is used to remove it from the staging area. It sounds strange, but Git can do it. Consider the below scenario:

We have deleted the newfile3.txt from the repository. The status of the repository after deleting the file is as follows:

```
HiMaNshU@HiMaNshU-PC MINGW64 ~/Desktop/NewDirectory (master)
$ git status
On branch master

No commits yet

Changes to be committed:
  (use "git rm --cached <file>..." to unstage)
        new file:   newfile.txt
        new file:   newfile1.txt
        new file:   newfile2.txt
        new file:   newfile3.txt

Changes not staged for commit:
  (use "git add/rm <file>..." to update what will be committed)
  (use "git restore <file>..." to discard changes in working directory
)
        deleted:    newfile3.txt
```

As we can see from the above output, the deleted file is still available in the staging area. To remove it from the index, run the below command as follows:

```
$ git add newfile3.txt
```

Consider the below output:

```
HiMaNshU@HiMaNshU-PC MINGW64 ~/Desktop/NewDirectory (master)
$ git add newfile3.txt

HiMaNshU@HiMaNshU-PC MINGW64 ~/Desktop/NewDirectory (master)
$ git status
on branch master

No commits yet

changes to be committed:
  (use "git rm --cached <file>..." to unstage)
        new file:   newfile.txt
        new file:   newfile1.txt
        new file:   newfile2.txt
```

From the above output, we can see that the file is removed from the staging area.

Add all New and Updated Files Only:
Git allows us to stage only updated and newly created files at once. We will use the ignore removal option to do so. It will be used as follows:

```
$ git add --ignore-removal .
```

Add all Modified and Deleted Files
Git add facilitates us with a variety of options. There is another option that is available in Git, which allows us to stage only the modified and deleted files. It will not stage the newly created file. To stage all modified and deleted files only, run the below command:

```
$ git add -u
```

Add Files by Wildcard
Git allows us to add all the same pattern files at once. It is another way to add multiple files together. Suppose I want to add all java files

or text files, then we can use pattern .java or .txt. To do so, we will run the command as follows:

```
$ git add *.java
```

The above command will stage all the Java files. The same pattern will be applied for the text files.

The next step after adding files is committing to share it on Git.

Git Undo Add

We can undo a git add operation. However, it is not a part of git add command, but we can do it through git reset command.

To undo an add operation, run the below command:

```
$ git reset <filename>
```

Git Commit

It is used to record the changes in the repository. It is the next command after the git add. Every commit contains the index data and the commit message. Every commit forms a parent-child relationship. When we add a file in Git, it will take place in the staging area. A commit command is used to fetch updates from the staging area to the repository.

The staging and committing are co-related to each other. Staging allows us to continue in making changes to the repository, and when we want to share these changes to the version control system, committing allows us to record these changes.

Commits are the snapshots of the project. Every commit is recorded in the master branch of the repository. We can recall the commits or revert it to the older version. Two different commits will never overwrite because each commit has its own commit-id. This commit-id is a cryptographic number created by SHA (Secure Hash Algorithm) algorithm.

Let's see the different kinds of commits.

The git commit command

The commit command will commit the changes and generate a commit-id. The commit command without any argument will open the default text editor and ask for the commit message. We can specify our commit message in this text editor. It will run as follows:

```
$ git commit
```

The above command will prompt a default editor and ask for a commit message. We have made a change to newfile1.txt and want it to commit it. It can be done as follows:

Consider the below output:

```
HiMaNshU@HiMaNshU-PC MINGW64 ~/Desktop/NewDirectory (master)
$ git commit
[master e3107d8] Update Newfile1
 2 files changed, 1 insertion(+)
 delete mode 100644 index.jsp
```

As we run the command, it will prompt a default text editor and ask for a commit message. The text editor will look like as follows:

```
Update Newfile1
# Please enter the commit message for your changes. Lines starting
# with '#' will be ignored, and an empty message aborts the commit.
#
# On branch master
# Changes to be committed:
#       deleted:    index.jsp
#       modified:   newfile1.txt
#
~
~
~
~
~
~
~
~
~
~
~
~
<U/Desktop/NewDirectory/.git/COMMIT_EDITMSG[+] [unix] (17:59 26/11/2019)1,15 All
:wq
```

Press the Esc key and after that 'I' for insert mode. Type a commit message whatever you want. Press Esc after that ':wq' to save and exit from the editor. Hence, we have successfully made a commit.

We can check the commit by git log command. Consider the below output:

```
HiMaNshU@HiMaNshU-PC MINGW64 ~/Desktop/NewDirectory (master)
$ git log
commit e3107d8c534e92dcc3c87a36afc8be9c274a87b5 (HEAD -> master)
Author: ImDwivedi1 <himanshudubey481@gmail.com>
Date:   Tue Nov 26 17:59:44 2019 +0530

    Update Newfile1
```

We can see in the above output that log option is displaying commit-id, author detail, date and time, and the commit message.

Git commit -a

The commit command also provides -a option to specify some commits. It is used to commit the snapshots of all changes. This option only consider already added files in Git. It will not commit the newly created files. Consider below scenario:

We have made some updates to our already staged file newfile3 and create a file newfile4.txt. Check the status of the repository and run the commit command as follows:

```
$ git commit -a
```

Consider the output:

```
HiMaNshU@HiMaNshU-PC MINGW64 ~/Desktop/NewDirectory (master)
$ touch newfile4.txt

HiMaNshU@HiMaNshU-PC MINGW64 ~/Desktop/NewDirectory (master)
$ git status
on branch master
changes not staged for commit:
  (use "git add <file>..." to update what will be committed)
  (use "git restore <file>..." to discard changes in working directory)
        modified:   newfile3.txt

untracked files:
  (use "git add <file>..." to include in what will be committed)
        newfile4.txt

no changes added to commit (use "git add" and/or "git commit -a")

HiMaNshU@HiMaNshU-PC MINGW64 ~/Desktop/NewDirectory (master)
$ git commit -a
[master fc66f84] updated newfile3
 1 file changed, 1 insertion(+)
```

The above command will prompt our default text editor and ask for the commit message. Type a commit message, and then save and exit from the editor. This process will only commit the already added files. It will not commit the files that have not been staged. Consider the below output:

```
HiMaNshU@HiMaNshU-PC MINGW64 ~/Desktop/NewDirectory (master)
$ git status
on branch master
untracked files:
  (use "git add <file>..." to include in what will be committed)
        newfile4.txt

nothing added to commit but untracked files present (use "git add" to
```

As we can see in the above output, the newfile4.txt has not been committed.

Git commit -m

The -m option of commit command lets you to write the commit message on the command line. This command will not prompt the text editor. It will run as follows:

```
$ git commit -m "Commit message."
```

The above command will make a commit with the given commit message. Consider the below output:

```
HiMaNshU@HiMaNshU-PC MINGW64 ~/Desktop/NewDirectory (master)
$ git commit -m "Introduced newfile4"
[master 64d1891] Introduced newfile4
 1 file changed, 0 insertions(+), 0 deletions(-)
 create mode 100644 newfile4.txt
```

In the above output, a newfile4.txt is committed to our repository with a commit message.

We can also use the -am option for already staged files. This command will immediately make a commit for already staged files with a commit message. It will run as follows:

```
$ git commit -am "Commit message."
```

Git Commit Amend (Change commit message)

The amend option lets us to edit the last commit. If accidentally, we have committed a wrong commit message, then this feature is a savage option for us. It will run as follows:

```
$ git commit -amend
```

The above command will prompt the default text editor and allow us to edit the commit message.

We may need some other essential operations related to commit like revert commit, undo a commit, and more, but these operations are not a part of the commit command. We can do it with other commands. Some essential operations are as follows:

- ❖ Git undo commit
- ❖ Git revert commit
- ❖ git remove commit

Git Clone

In Git, cloning is the act of making a copy of any target repository. The target repository can be remote or local. You can clone your repository from the remote repository to create a local copy on your system. Also, you can sync between the two locations.

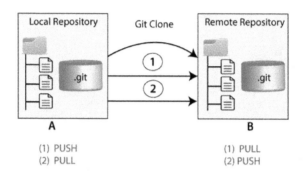

A

(1) PUSH
(2) PULL

B

(1) PULL
(2) PUSH

Git Clone Command

The git clone is a command-line utility which is used to make a local copy of a remote repository. It accesses the repository through a remote URL.

Usually, the original repository is located on a remote server, often from a Git service like GitHub, Bitbucket, or GitLab. The remote repository URL is referred to the origin.

Syntax:

```
$ git clone <repository URL>
```

Git Clone Repository

Suppose, you want to clone a repository from GitHub, or have an existing repository owned by any other user you would like to contribute. Steps to clone a repository are as follows:

Step 1: Open GitHub and navigate to the main page of the repository.

Step 2: Under the repository name, click on Clone or download.

Step 3: Select the Clone with HTTPs section and copy the clone URL for the repository. For the empty repository, you can copy the repository page URL from your browser and skip to next step.

Step 4: Open Git Bash and change the current working directory to your desired location where you want to create the local copy of the repository.

Step 5: Use the git clone command with repository URL to make a copy of the remote repository. See the below command:

```
$ git clone https://github.com/ImDwivedi1/Git-Example.git
```

Now, Press Enter. Hence, your local cloned repository will be created. See the below output:

```
HiMaNshU@HiMaNshU-PC MINGW64 ~/Desktop (master)
$ cd "new folder"

HiMaNshU@HiMaNshU-PC MINGW64 ~/Desktop/new folder (master)
$ git clone https://github.com/ImDwivedi1/Git-Example.git
Cloning into 'Git-Example'...
remote: Enumerating objects: 6, done.
remote: Counting objects: 100% (6/6), done.
remote: Compressing objects: 100% (4/4), done.
remote: Total 6 (delta 0), reused 0 (delta 0), pack-reused 0
Unpacking objects: 100% (6/6), done.

HiMaNshU@HiMaNshU-PC MINGW64 ~/Desktop/new folder (master)
$
```

Cloning a Repository into a Specific Local Folder

Git allows cloning the repository into a specific directory without switching to that particular directory. You can specify that directory as the next command-line argument in git clone command. See the below command:

```
$ git clone https://github.com/ImDwivedi1/Git-
Example.git "new folder(2)"
```

```
HiMaNshU@HiMaNshU-PC MINGW64 ~/Desktop (master)
$ git clone https://github.com/ImDwivedi1/Git-Example.git "new folder(2)"
Cloning into 'new folder(2)'...
remote: Enumerating objects: 6, done.
remote: Counting objects: 100% (6/6), done.
remote: Compressing objects: 100% (4/4), done.
remote: Total 6 (delta 0), reused 0 (delta 0), pack-reused 0
Unpacking objects: 100% (6/6), done.

HiMaNshU@HiMaNshU-PC MINGW64 ~/Desktop (master)
$
```

The given command does the same thing as the previous one, but the target directory is switched to the specified directory.

Git has another transfer protocol called SSH protocol. The above example uses the git:// protocol, but you can also use http(s):// or user@server:/path.git, which uses the SSH transfer protocol.

Git Clone Branch

Git allows making a copy of only a particular branch from a repository. You can make a directory for the individual branch by using the git clone command. To make a clone branch, you need to specify the branch name with -b command. Below is the syntax of the command to clone the specific git branch:

Syntax:

```
$ git clone -b <Branch name><Repository URL>
```

See the below command:

```
$ git clone -b master https://github.com/ImDwivedi1/Git-Example.git "new folder(2)"
```

```
HiManShU@HiManShU-PC MINGW64 ~/Desktop/new folder(2) (master)
$ git clone -b master https://github.com/ImDwivedi1/Git-Example.git
Cloning into 'Git-Example'...
remote: Enumerating objects: 9, done.
remote: Counting objects: 100% (9/9), done.
remote: Compressing objects: 100% (6/6), done.
remote: Total 9 (delta 1), reused 0 (delta 0), pack-reused 0
Unpacking objects: 100% (9/9), done.

HiManShU@HiManShU-PC MINGW64 ~/Desktop/new folder(2) (master)
$ |
```

In the given output, only the master branch is cloned from the principal repository Git-Example.

Git Stash

Sometimes you want to switch the branches, but you are working on an incomplete part of your current project. You don't want to make a commit of half-done work. Git stashing allows you to do so. The git stash command enables you to switch branches without committing the current branch.

The below figure demonstrates the properties and role of stashing concerning repository and working directory.

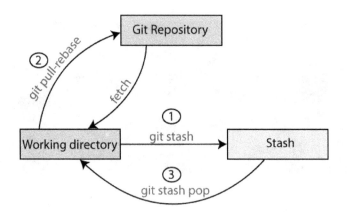

Generally, the stash's meaning is "store something safely in a hidden place." The sense in Git is also the same for stash; Git temporarily saves your data safely without committing.

Stashing takes the messy state of your working directory, and temporarily save it for further use. Many options are available with git stash. Some useful options are given below:

- ❖ Git stash
- ❖ Git stash save
- ❖ Git stash list
- ❖ Git stash apply
- ❖ Git stash changes
- ❖ Git stash pop
- ❖ Git stash drop
- ❖ Git stash clear
- ❖ Git stash branch

Stashing Work

Let's understand it with a real-time scenario. I have made changes to my project GitExample2 in two files from two distinct branches. I am in a messy state, and I have not entirely edited any file yet. So I want to save it temporarily for future use. We can stash it to save as its current status. To stash, let's have a look at the repository's current status. To check the current status of the repository, run the git status command. The git status command is used as:

Syntax:

```
$ git status
```

Output:

```
HiMaNshU@HiMaNshU-PC MINGW64 ~/Desktop/GitExample2 (test)
$ git status
On branch test
Changes not staged for commit:
  (use "git add <file>..." to update what will be committed)
  (use "git restore <file>..." to discard changes in working directory)
        modified:   design.css
        modified:   newfile.txt

no changes added to commit (use "git add" and/or "git commit -a")
```

From the above output, you can see the status that there are two untracked file design.css and newfile.txt available in the repository. To save it temporarily, we can use the git stash command. The git stash command is used as:

Syntax:

```
$ git stash
```

```
HiMaNshU@HiMaNshU-PC MINGW64 ~/Desktop/GitExample2 (test)
$ git stash
Saved working directory and index state WIP on test: 0a1a475 CSS file
```

In the given output, the work is saved with git stash command. We can check the status of the repository.

```
HiMaNshU@HiMaNshU-PC MINGW64 ~/Desktop/GitExample2 (test)
$ git status
On branch test
nothing to commit, working tree clean
```

As you can see, my work is just stashed in its current position. Now, the directory is cleaned. At this point, you can switch between branches and work on them.

Git Stash Save (Saving Stashes with the message):

In Git, the changes can be stashed with a message. To stash a change with a message, run the below command:

Syntax:

```
$ git stash save "<Stashing Message>"
```

Output:

```
HiMaNshU@HiMaNshU-PC MINGW64 ~/Desktop/GitExample2 (test)
$ git stash save "Edited both files"
Saved working directory and index state On test: Edited both files
```

The above stash will be saved with a message

Git Stash List (Check the Stored Stashes)

To check the stored stashes, run the below command:

Syntax:

```
$ git stash list
```

Output:

```
HiMaNshU@HiMaNshU-PC MINGW64 ~/Desktop/GitExample2 (test)
$ git stash list
stash@{0}: WIP on test: 0a1a475 CSS file

HiMaNshU@HiMaNshU-PC MINGW64 ~/Desktop/GitExample2 (test)
$
```

In the above case, I have made one stash, which is displayed as "stash@{0}: WIP on the test: 0a1a475 CSS file".

If we have more than one stash, then It will display all the stashes respectively with different stash id. Consider the below output:

```
HiMaNshU@HiMaNshU-PC MINGW64 ~/Desktop/GitExample2 (test)
$ git stash list
stash@{0}: On test: Edited both files
stash@{1}: WIP on test: 0a1a475 CSS file
```

It will show all the stashes with indexing as stash@{0}: stash@{1}: and so on.

Git Stash Apply

You can re-apply the changes that you just stashed by using the git stash command. To apply the commit, use the git stash command, followed by the apply option. It is used as:

Syntax:

```
$ git stash apply
```

Output:

```
HiMaNshU@HiMaNshU-PC MINGW64 ~/Desktop/GitExample2 (test)
$ git stash apply
on branch test
Changes not staged for commit:
  (use "git add <file>..." to update what will be committed)
  (use "git restore <file>..." to discard changes in working directory
)
        modified:   design.css
        modified:   newfile.txt

no changes added to commit (use "git add" and/or "git commit -a")
```

The above output restores the last stash. Now, if you will check the status of the repository, it will show the changes that are made on the file. Consider the below output:

q

```
HiMaNshU@HiMaNshU-PC MINGW64 ~/Desktop/GitExample2 (test)
$ git status
on branch test
Changes not staged for commit:
  (use "git add <file>..." to update what will be committed)
  (use "git restore <file>..." to discard changes in working directory
)
        modified:   design.css
        modified:   newfile.txt

no changes added to commit (use "git add" and/or "git commit -a")
```

From the above output, you can see that the repository is restored to its previous state before stash. It is showing output as "Changes not staged for commit."

In case of more than one stash, you can use "git stash apply" command followed by stash index id to apply the particular commit. It is used as:

Syntax:

$ git stash apply <stash id>

Consider the below output:

Output:

```
HiMaNshU@HiMaNshU-PC MINGW64 ~/Desktop/GitExample2 (test)
$ git stash apply stash@{1}
error: Your local changes to the following files would be overwritten b
y merge:
        design.css
        newfile.txt
Please commit your changes or stash them before you merge.
Aborting
```

If we don't specify a stash, Git takes the most recent stash and tries to apply it.

Git Stash Changes

We can track the stashes and their changes. To see the changes in the file before stash and after stash operation, run the below command:

Syntax:

```
$ git stash show
```

The above command will show the file that is stashed and changes made on them. Consider the below output:

Output:

```
HiMaNShU@HiMaNShU-PC MINGW64 ~/Desktop/GitExample2 (test)
$ git stash show
 design.css  | 1 +
 newfile.txt | 1 +
 2 files changed, 2 insertions(+)
```

The above output illustrates that there are two files that are stashed, and two insertions performed on them.

We can exactly track what changes are made on the file. To display the changed content of the file, perform the below command:

Syntax:

```
$ git stash show -p
```

Here, -p stands for the partial stash. The given command will show the edited files and content, consider the following output:

```
HiMaNshU@HiMaNshU-PC MINGW64 ~/Desktop/GitExample2 (test)
$ git stash show -p
diff --git a/design.css b/design.css
index 32bebd0..645450f 100644
--- a/design.css
+++ b/design.css
@@ -42,6 +42,7 @@ label
 {
        font-size:30px;
        color:blue;
+font:size;^M

 }
 .second
diff --git a/newfile.txt b/newfile.txt
index d411be5..9e913d4 100644
--- a/newfile.txt
+++ b/newfile.txt
@@ -1,2 +1,3 @@
 new file to check git Head
 NEW COMMIT IN MASTER BRANCH.
+asdvajhsgdfkaseg
```

The above output is showing the file name with changed content. It acts the same as git diff command. The git diff command will also show the exact output.

Git Stash Pop (Reapplying Stashed Changes)

Git allows the user to re-apply the previous commits by using git stash pop command. The popping option removes the changes from stash and applies them to your working file.

The git stash pop command is quite similar to git stash apply. The main difference between both of these commands is stash pop command that deletes the stash from the stack after it is applied.

Syntax:

```
$ git stash pop
```

The above command will re-apply the previous commits to the repository. Consider the below output.

Output:

```
HiMaNshU@HiMaNshU-PC MINGW64 ~/Desktop/GitExample2 (master)
$ git stash pop
On branch master
changes not staged for commit:
  (use "git add <file>..." to update what will be committed)
  (use "git restore <file>..." to discard changes in working directory)
        modified:   newfile.txt

no changes added to commit (use "git add" and/or "git commit -a")
Dropped refs/stash@{0} (55eb409b4135a9d378a6bd2e27940f405164573a)
```

Git Stash Drop (Unstash)

The git stash drop command is used to delete a stash from the queue. Generally, it deletes the most recent stash. Caution should be taken before using stash drop command, as it is difficult to undo if once applied.

The only way to revert it is if you do not close the terminal after deleting the stash. The stash drop command will be used as:

Syntax:

```
$ git stash drop
```

Output:

```
HiMaNshU@HiMaNshU-PC MINGW64 ~/Desktop/GitExample2 (master)
$ git stash list
stash@{0}: WIP on master: 56afce0 Added an empty newfile2
stash@{1}: WIP on master: 56afce0 Added an empty newfile2
stash@{2}: WIP on test: 0a1a475 CSS file

HiMaNshU@HiMaNshU-PC MINGW64 ~/Desktop/GitExample2 (master)
$ git stash drop
Dropped refs/stash@{0} (a9dc6ba6847ebcd2a69c16693359b516e6e8c3d9)

HiMaNshU@HiMaNshU-PC MINGW64 ~/Desktop/GitExample2 (master)
$ git stash list
stash@{0}: WIP on master: 56afce0 Added an empty newfile2
stash@{1}: WIP on test: 0a1a475 CSS file
```

In the above output, the most recent stash (stash@{0}) has been dropped from given three stashes. The stash list command lists all the available stashes in the queue.

We can also delete a particular stash from the queue. To delete a particular stash from the available stashes, pass the stash id in stash drop command. It will be processed as:

Syntax:

```
$ git stash drop <stash id>
```

Assume that I have two stashes available in my queue, and I don't want to drop my most recent stash, but I want to delete the older one. Then, it will be operated as:

```
$ git stash drop stash@{1}
```

Consider the below output:

```
HiMaNshU@HiMaNshU-PC MINGW64 ~/Desktop/GitExample2 (master)
$ git stash drop stash@{1}
Dropped stash@{1} (90d7c9ab35bcd951f43cbfe863293555c7df727b)

HiMaNshU@HiMaNshU-PC MINGW64 ~/Desktop/GitExample2 (master)
$ git stash list
stash@{0}: WIP on master: 56afce0 Added an empty newfile2
```

In the above output, the commit stash@{1} has been deleted from the queue.

Git Stash Clear

The git stash clear command allows deleting all the available stashes at once. To delete all the available stashes, operate below command:

Syntax:

```
$ git stash clear
```

it will delete all the stashes that exist in the repository.

Output:

```
HiMaNshU@HiMaNshU-PC MINGW64 ~/Desktop/GitExample2 (master)
$ git stash clear

HiMaNshU@HiMaNshU-PC MINGW64 ~/Desktop/GitExample2 (master)
$ git stash list

HiMaNshU@HiMaNshU-PC MINGW64 ~/Desktop/GitExample2 (master)
$
```

All the stashes are deleted in the above output. The git stash list command is blank because there are no stashes available in the repository.

Git Stash Branch

If you stashed some work on a particular branch and continue working on that branch. Then, it may create a conflict during merging. So, it is good to stash work on a separate branch.

The git stash branch command allows the user to stash work on a separate branch to avoid conflicts. The syntax for this branch is as follows:

Syntax:

```
$ git stash branch <Branch Name>
```

The above command will create a new branch and transfer the stashed work on that. Consider the below output:

Output:

```
HiMaNshU@HiMaNshU-PC MINGW64 ~/Desktop/GitExample2 (master)
$ git stash save "Demo for stash Branch"
Saved working directory and index state On master: Demo for stash Branch

HiMaNshU@HiMaNshU-PC MINGW64 ~/Desktop/GitExample2 (master)
$ git stash branch testing
Switched to a new branch 'testing'
on branch testing
```

In the above output, the stashed work is transferred to a newly created branch testing. It will avoid the merge conflict on the master branch.

Git Ignore

In Git, the term "ignore" is used to specify intentionally untracked files that Git should ignore. It doesn't affect the Files that already tracked by Git.

Sometimes you don't want to send the files to Git service like GitHub. We can specify files in Git to ignore.

The file system of Git is classified into three categories:

❖ Tracked: Tracked files are such files that are previously staged or committed.
❖ Untracked: Untracked files are such files that are not previously staged or committed.
❖ Ignored: Ignored files are such files that are explicitly ignored by git. We have to tell git to ignore such files.

Generally, the Ignored files are artifacts and machine-generated files. These files can be derived from your repository source or should otherwise not be committed. Some commonly ignored files are as follows:

❖ dependency caches
❖ compiled code
❖ build output directories, like /bin, /out, or /target
❖ runtime file generated, like .log, .lock, or .tmp
❖ Hidden system files, like Thumbs.db or.DS_Store
❖ Personal IDE config files, such as .idea/workspace.xml

Git Ignore Files

Git ignore files is a file that can be any file or a folder that contains all the files that we want to ignore. The developers ignore files that are not necessary to execute the project. Git itself creates many system-generated ignored files. Usually, these files are hidden files. There are several ways to specify the ignore files. The ignored files can be tracked on a .gitignore file that is placed on the root folder of the repository. No explicit command is used to ignore the file.

There is no explicit git ignore command; instead, the .gitignore file must be edited and committed by hand when you have new files that you wish to ignore. The .gitignore files hold patterns that are matched against file names in your repository to determine whether or not they should be ignored.

How to Ignore Files Manually

There is no command in Git to ignore files; alternatively, there are several ways to specify the ignore files in git. One of the most common ways is the .gitignore file. Let's understand it with an example.

The .gitignore file:

Rules for ignoring file is defined in the .gitignore file. The .gitignore file is a file that contains all the formats and files of the ignored file. We can create multiple ignore files in a different directory. Let's understand how it works with an example:

Step1: Create a file named .gitignore if you do not have it already in your directory. To create a file, use the command touch or cat. It will use as follows:

```
$ touch .gitignore
```

Or

```
$ cat .gitignore
```

The above command will create a .gitignore file on your directory. Remember, you are working on your desired directory. Consider the below command:

```
HiMaNshU@HiMaNshU-PC MINGW64 ~/Desktop/GitExample2 (test2)
$ touch .gitignore
```

The above command will create a file named .gitignored. We can track it on the repository. Consider the following image:

Name	Date modified	Type	Size
.git	11/5/2019 11:33 AM	File folder	
New folder	11/5/2019 11:31 AM	File folder	
.gitignore	11/5/2019 11:32 AM	Text Document	1 KB
design.css	10/15/2019 2:07 PM	Cascading Style S...	1 KB
index.jsp	9/19/2019 6:10 PM	JSP File	2 KB
master.jsp	9/19/2019 6:10 PM	JSP File	1 KB
merge the branch	9/20/2019 6:05 PM	File	1 KB
newfile.txt	10/15/2019 2:20 PM	Text Document	1 KB
newfile1.txt	10/15/2019 2:27 PM	Text Document	1 KB
newfile2.txt	11/3/2019 5:22 PM	Text Document	1 KB
README.md	9/19/2019 6:10 PM	MD File	1 KB

As you can see from the above image, a .gitignore file has been created for my repository.

Step2: Now, add the files and directories to the .gitignore file that you want to ignore. To add the files and directory to the .git ignore the file, open the file and type the file name, directory name, and pattern to ignore files and directories. Consider the below image:

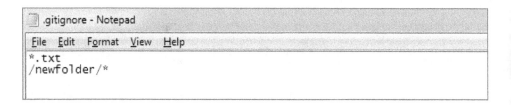

In the above file, I have given one format and a directory to ignore. The above format *.txt will ignore all the text files from the repository, and /newfolder/* will ignore the newfolder and its sub-content. We can also give only the name of any file to ignore.

Step3: Now, to share it on Git, we have to commit it. The .gitignore file is still now in staging area; we can track it by git status command. Consider the following output:

```
HiMaNshU@HiMaNshU-PC MINGW64 ~/Desktop/GitExample2 (test2)
$ git status
on branch test2
changes to be committed:
  (use "git restore --staged <file>..." to unstage)
      modified:   newfile2.txt

untracked files:
  (use "git add <file>..." to include in what will be committed)
      .gitignore
```

Now to stage it, we have to commit it. To commit it, run the below command:

$ git add .gitignore

$ git commit -m "ignored directory created."

The above command will share the file .gitignore on Git. Consider the below output.

```
HiMaNshU@HiMaNshU-PC MINGW64 ~/Desktop/GitExample2 (test2)
$ git add .gitignore

HiMaNshU@HiMaNshU-PC MINGW64 ~/Desktop/GitExample2 (test2)
$ git commit -m " ignored directory created"
[test2 9d9470e]  ignored directory created
 2 files changed, 2 insertions(+)
 create mode 100644 .gitignore
```

Now, we have ignored a pattern file and a directory in Git.

Rules for putting the pattern in .gitignore file:

The rules for the patterns that can be put in the .gitignore file are as follows:

❖ Git ignores the Blank lines or lines starting with #.
❖ Only the Standard glob patterns work and will be applied recursively throughout the entire working tree.
❖ The patterns can be started with a forward slash (/) to avoid recursively.
❖ The patterns can be ended with a forward slash (/) to specify a directory.
❖ The patterns can be negated by starting it with an exclamation point (!).

Global .gitignore:.

As we know that we can create multiple .gitignore files for a project. But Git also allows us to create a universal .gitignore file that can be used for the whole project. This file is known as a global .gitignore file. To create a global .gitignore, run the below command on terminal:

```
$ git config --global core.excludesfile ~/.gitignore_global
```

The above command will create a global .gitignore file for the repository.

How to List the Ignored Files?

In Git, We can list the ignored files. There are various commands to list the ignored files, but the most common way to list the file is the ls command. To list the ignored file, run the ls command as follows:

```
$ git ls-files -i --exclude-standard
```

Or

```
$ git ls-files --ignore --exclude-standard
```

The above command will list all available ignored files from the repository. In the given command, -I option stands for ignore and --exclude-standard is specifying the exclude pattern. Consider the below output:

```
HiMaNShU@HiMaNShU-PC MINGW64 ~/Desktop/GitExample2 (test2)
$ git ls-files -i --exclude-standard
newfile.txt
newfile1.txt
newfile2.txt
```

From the above output, we can see that the ls command is listing the available ignored files from the repository.

Git Fork

A fork is a rough copy of a repository. Forking a repository allows you to freely test and debug with changes without affecting the original project. One of the excessive use of forking is to propose changes for bug fixing. To resolve an issue for a bug that you found, you can:

❖ Fork the repository.
❖ Make the fix.
❖ Forward a pull request to the project owner.

Forking is not a Git function; it is a feature of Git service like GitHub.

When to Use Git Fork

Generally, forking a repository allows us to experiment on the project without affecting the original project. Following are the reasons for forking the repository:

❖ Propose changes to someone else's project.
❖ Use an existing project as a starting point.

Let's understand how to fork a repository on GitHub?

How to Fork a Repository?
The forking and branching are excellent ways to contribute to an open-source project. These two features of Git allows the enhanced collaboration on the projects.

Forking is a safe way to contribute. It allows us to make a rough copy of the project. We can freely experiment on the project. After the final version of the project, we can create a pull request for merging.

It is a straight-forward process. Steps for forking the repository are as follows:

❖ Login to the GitHub account.
❖ Find the GitHub repository which you want to fork.
❖ Click the Fork button on the upper right side of the repository's page.

We can't fork our own repository. Only shared repositories can be fork. If someone wants to fork the repository, then he must log in with his account. Let's understand the below scenario in which a user pune2016 wants to contribute to our project GitExample2. When he searches or put the address of our repository, our repository will look like as follows:

The above image shows the user interface of my repository from other contributors. We can see the fork option at the top right corner of the repository page. By clicking on that, the forking process will start. It will take a while to make a copy of the project for other users. After the forking completed, a copy of the repository will be copied to your GitHub account. It will not affect the original repository. We can freely make changes and then create a pull request for the main project. The owner of the project will see your suggestion and decide whether he wants to merge the changes or not. The fork copy will look like as follows:

As you can see, the forked repository looks like pune2016/GitExample2. At the bottom of the repository name, we can see a description of the repository. At the top right corner, the option fork is increased by 1 number.

Hence one can fork the repository from GitHub.

Fork vs. Clone
Sometimes people considered the fork as clone command because of their property. Both commands are used to create another copy of the repository. But the significant difference is that the fork is used to

create a server-side copy, and clone is used to create a local copy of the repository.

There is no particular command for forking the repository; instead, it is a service provided by third-party Git service like GitHub. Comparatively, git clone is a command-line utility that is used to create a local copy of the project.

Generally, people working on the same project clone the repository and the external contributors fork the repository.

A pull request can merge the changes made on the fork repository. We can create a pull request to propose changes to the project. Comparatively, changes made on the cloned repository can be merged by pushing. We can push the changes to our remote repository.

Git Repository

In Git, the repository is like a data structure used by VCS to store metadata for a set of files and directories. It contains the collection of the files as well as the history of changes made to those files. Repository in Git is considered as your project folder. A repository has all the project-related data. Distinct projects have distinct repositories.

Getting a Git Repository

There are two ways to obtain a repository. They are as follows:

- ❖ Create a local repository and make it as Git repository.
- ❖ Clone a remote repository (already exists on a server).

In either case, you can start working on a Git repository.

Initializing a Repository

If you want to share your project on a version control system and control it with Git. Then, browse your project's directory and start the git command line (Git Bash for Windows) here. To initialize a new repository, run the below command:

Syntax:

```
$ git init
```
Output:

```
HiMaNshU@HiMaNshU-PC MINGW64 /c/My Project
$ git init
Initialized empty Git repository in C:/My Project/.git/

HiMaNshU@HiMaNshU-PC MINGW64 /c/My Project (master)
$ |
```

The above command will create a new subdirectory named .git that holds all necessary repository files. The .git subdirectory can be understood as a Git repository skeleton. Consider the below image:

.git	10/12/2019 4:04 PM	File folder		
design	9/19/2019 6:10 PM	Cascading Style S...	1 KB	
design2	10/6/2019 5:21 PM	Cascading Style S...	1 KB	
index	9/19/2019 6:10 PM	JSP File	2 KB	
master	9/19/2019 6:10 PM	JSP File	1 KB	
merge the branch	9/20/2019 6:05 PM	File	1 KB	
newfile	10/4/2019 2:10 PM	Text Document	1 KB	
newfile1	10/4/2019 2:10 PM	Text Document	1 KB	
newfile2	10/9/2019 12:26 PM	Text Document	0 KB	
README	9/19/2019 6:10 PM	MD File	1 KB	

An empty repository .git is added to my existing project. If we want to start version-controlling for existing files, we should track these files with git add command, followed by a commit.

We can list all the untracked files by git status command.

```
$ git status
```
Consider the below output:

```
HiMaNshU@HiMaNshU-PC MINGW64 /c/My Project (master)
$ git status
On branch master

No commits yet

Untracked files:
  (use "git add <file>..." to include in what will be committed)
        README.md
        design.css
        design2.css
        index.jsp
        master.jsp
        merge the branch
        newfile.txt
        newfile1.txt
        newfile2.txt

nothing added to commit but untracked files present (use "git add" to track)
```

In the above output, the list of all untracked files is displayed by the git status command. To share these files on the version control system, we have to track it with git add command followed by a commit. To track the files, operate git add command as follows:

Syntax:

```
$ git add <filename>
```

To commit a file, perform the git commit command as follows:

```
$ git commit -m "Commit message."
```

Output:

```
HiMaNshU@HiMaNshU-PC MINGW64 /c/My Project (master)
$ git add design.css

HiMaNshU@HiMaNshU-PC MINGW64 /c/My Project (master)
$ git add design2.css

HiMaNshU@HiMaNshU-PC MINGW64 /c/My Project (master)
$ git add index.jsp

HiMaNshU@HiMaNshU-PC MINGW64 /c/My Project (master)
$ git commit -m "added index and CSS file"
[master (root-commit) caac6fb] added index and CSS file
 3 files changed, 94 insertions(+)
 create mode 100644 design.css
 create mode 100644 design2.css
 create mode 100644 index.jsp
```

In the above output, I have added three of my existing files by git add command and commit it for sharing.

We can also create new files. To share the new file, follow the same procedure as described above; add and commit it for sharing. Now, you have a repository to share.

Cloning an Existing Repository

We can clone an existing repository. Suppose we have a repository on a version control system like subversion, GitHub, or any other remote server, and we want to share it with someone to contribute. The git clone command will make a copy for any user to contribute.

We can get nearly all data from server with git clone command. It can be done as:

```
$ git clone <Repository URL>
```

Suppose one of my friends has a repository on my GitHub account, and I want to contribute to it. So the first thing I will do, make a copy of this project to my local system for a better work interface. The essential element needed for cloning the repository URL. I have a repository URL "https://github.com/ImDwivedi1/Git-Example". To clone this repository, operate the clone command as:

```
$ git clone https://github.com/ImDwivedi1/Git-Example
```

Consider the below output:

```
HiMaNshU@HiMaNshU-PC MINGW64 ~/Desktop/Demo (master)
$ git clone https://github.com/ImDwivedi1/Git-Example
Cloning into 'Git-Example'...
remote: Enumerating objects: 23, done.
remote: Counting objects: 100% (23/23), done.
remote: Compressing objects: 100% (18/18), done.
remote: Total 23 (delta 5), reused 6 (delta 1), pack-reused 0
Unpacking objects: 100% (23/23), done.

HiMaNshU@HiMaNshU-PC MINGW64 ~/Desktop/Demo (master)
$ |
```

In the above output, the repository Git-Example has been cloned. Now this repository is available on your local storage. You can commit it and contribute to the project by pushing it on a remote server.

A single repository can be cloned any number of times. So we can clone a repository on various locations and various systems.

Git Index

The Git index is a staging area between the working directory and repository. It is used to build up a set of changes that you want to commit together. To better understand the Git index, then first understand the working directory and repository.

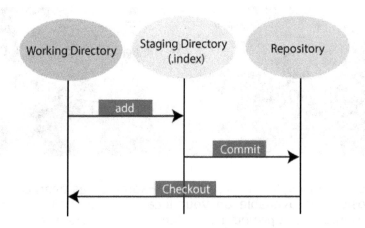

There are three places in Git where file changes can reside, and these are working directory, staging area, and the repository. To better understand the Git index first, let's take a quick view of these places.

Working directory:

When you worked on your project and made some changes, you are dealing with your project's working directory. This project directory is available on your computer's filesystem. All the changes you make will remain in the working directory until you add them to the staging area.

Staging area:

The staging area can be described as a preview of your next commit. When you create a git commit, Git takes changes that are in the staging area and make them as a new commit. You are allowed to add and remove changes from the staging area. The staging area can be considered as a real area where git stores the changes.

Although, Git doesn't have a dedicated staging directory where it can store some objects representing file changes (blobs). Instead of this, it uses a file called index.

Repository:

In Git, Repository is like a data structure used by GIt to store metadata for a set of files and directories. It contains the collection of the files as well as the history of changes made to those files. Repositories in Git is considered as your project folder. A repository has all the project-related data. Distinct projects have distinct repositories.

You can check what is in the index by the git status command. The git status command allows you to see which files are staged, modified but not yet staged, and completely untracked. Staged files mean, it is currently in the index. See the below example.

Syntax:

```
$ git status
```
Output:

```
HiMaNshU@HiMaNshU-PC MINGW64 ~/Desktop/GitExample2 (master)
$ git status
On branch master
Your branch is up to date with 'origin/master'.

Changes to be committed:
  (use "git restore --staged <file>..." to unstage)
        new file:   newfile.txt


HiMaNshU@HiMaNshU-PC MINGW64 ~/Desktop/GitExample2 (master)
```

In the given output, the status command shows the index.

As we mentioned earlier index is a file, not a directory, So Git is not storing objects into it. Instead, it stores information about each file in our repository. This information could be:

- ❖ mtime: It is the time of the last update.
- ❖ file: It is the name of the file.
- ❖ Wdir: The version of the file in the working directory.
- ❖ Stage: The version of the file in the index.
- ❖ Repo: The version of the file in the repository.

And finally, Git creates your working directory to match the content of the commit that HEAD is pointing.

Git Head

The HEAD points out the last commit in the current checkout branch. It is like a pointer to any reference. The HEAD can be understood as the "current branch." When you switch branches with 'checkout,' the HEAD is transferred to the new branch.

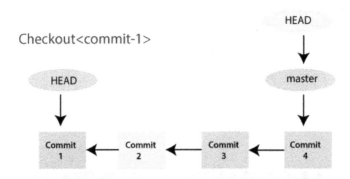

The above fig shows the HEAD referencing commit-1 because of a 'checkout' was done at commit-1. When you make a new commit, it shifts to the newer commit. The git head command is used to view the status of Head with different arguments. It stores the status of Head in .git\refs\heads directory. Let's see the below example:

Git Show Head

The git show head is used to check the status of the Head. This command will show the location of the Head.

Syntax:

```
$ git show HEAD
```
Output:

```
HiMaNshU@HiMaNshU-PC MINGW64 ~/Desktop/GitExample2 (edited)
$ git show HEAD
commit 00fcce523529c269692271f406baf828a5112230 (HEAD -> edited, origin/edited)
Author: ImDwivedi1 <52317024+ImDwivedi1@users.noreply.github.com>
Date:   Sat Sep 14 16:46:19 2019 +0530

    Update Index.jsp

    you have not mentioned the contact info, so i have edited this file.

diff --git a/index.jsp b/index.jsp
index 371223b..236e116 100644
--- a/index.jsp
+++ b/index.jsp
@@ -27,4 +27,6 @@
```

In the above output, you can see that the commit id for the Head is given. It means the Head is on the given commit.

Now, check the commit history of the project. You can use the git log command to check the commit history. See the below output:

```
HiMaNshU@HiMaNshU-PC MINGW64 ~/Desktop/GitExample2 (edited)
$ git log
commit 00fcce523529c269692271f406baf828a5112230 (HEAD -> edited, origin/edited)
Author: ImDwivedi1 <52317024+ImDwivedi1@users.noreply.github.com>
Date:   Sat Sep 14 16:46:19 2019 +0530

    Update Index.jsp

    you have not mentioned the contact info, so i have edited this file.

commit 4a6693a71151323623c04dd75cb0d44c1c4dbadf (origin/master, origin/HEAD)
Merge: 30193f3 78c5fbd
Author: ImDwivedi1 <52317024+ImDwivedi1@users.noreply.github.com>
Date:   Mon Sep 9 15:24:13 2019 +0530

    Merge pull request #1 from ImDwivedi1/branch2

    Create merge the branch
```

As we can see in the above output, the commit id for most recent commit and Head is the same. So, it is clear that the last commit has the Head.

We can also check the status of the Head by the commit id. Copy the commit id from the above output and paste it with the git show command. Its result is same as git show head command if the commit id is last commit's id. See the below output:

```
HiMaNshU@HiMaNshU-PC MINGW64 ~/Desktop/GitExample2 (edited)
$ git show 00fcce523529c269692271f406baf828a5112230
commit 00fcce523529c269692271f406baf828a5112230 (HEAD -> edited, origin/edited)
Author: ImDwivedi1 <52317024+ImDwivedi1@users.noreply.github.com>
Date:   Sat Sep 14 16:46:19 2019 +0530

    Update Index.jsp

    you have not mentioned the contact info, so i have edited this file.

diff --git a/index.jsp b/index.jsp
index 371223b..236e116 100644
--- a/index.jsp
+++ b/index.jsp
@@ -27,4 +27,6 @@
```

The above output is the same as git show output.

The HEAD is capable of referring to a specific revision that is not associated with a branch name. This situation is called a detached HEAD.

Git Detached Head

GitHub keeps track of all commits or snapshots over time. If you check the 'git log' in your terminal, you can show all the previous commits up to the first commit. Detached HEAD mode allows you to discover an older state of a repository. It is a natural state in Git.

When Head doesn't point to most recent commit, such state is called detached Head. If you checkout with an older commit, it will stand the detached head condition. See the following example:

```
HiMaNshU@HiMaNshU-PC MINGW64 ~/Desktop/Gitexample2 (master)
$ git log
commit 4a6693a71151323623c04dd75cb0d44c1c4dbadf (HEAD -> master, origin/master,
origin/HEAD, test)
Merge: 30193f3 78c5fbd
Author: ImDwivedi1 <52317024+ImDwivedi1@users.noreply.github.com>
Date:   Mon Sep 9 15:24:13 2019 +0530

    Merge pull request #1 from ImDwivedi1/branch2

    Create merge the branch

commit 30193f39dc8656ed7417500e3ffa3d16d049cb01
Author: ImDwivedi1 <52317024+ImDwivedi1@users.noreply.github.com>
Date:   Mon Sep 9 15:23:29 2019 +0530

    new files via upload

commit 78c5fbdab6d330f14d3e44d4703f887d6cd0e827
Author: ImDwivedi1 <52317024+ImDwivedi1@users.noreply.github.com>
Date:   Fri Aug 30 16:28:38 2019 +0530

    Create merge the branch
```

I have copied the older commit id. Now I will check out with this id.

```
HiMaNshU@HiMaNshU-PC MINGW64 ~/Desktop/GitExample2 (master)
$ git checkout 30193f39dc8656ed7417500e3ffa3d16d049cb01
Note: switching to '30193f39dc8656ed7417500e3ffa3d16d049cb01'.

You are in 'detached HEAD' state. You can look around, make experimental
changes and commit them, and you can discard any commits you make in this
state without impacting any branches by switching back to a branch.

If you want to create a new branch to retain commits you create, you may
do so (now or later) by using -c with the switch command. Example:

  git switch -c <new-branch-name>

Or undo this operation with:

  git switch -

Turn off this advice by setting config variable advice.detachedHead to false

HEAD is now at 30193f3 new files via upload
A       newfile.txt
```

As you can see in the given example, Head does not point the most recent commit. It is called a detached head state. It is always recommended, do not commit on detached Head.

Git Origin Master

The term "git origin master" is used in the context of a remote repository. It is used to deal with the remote repository. The term origin comes from where repository original situated and master stands for the main branch. Let's understand both of these terms in detail.

Git Master

Master is a naming convention for Git branch. It's a default branch of Git. After cloning a project from a remote server, the resulting local repository contains only a single local branch. This branch is called a "master" branch. It means that "master" is a repository's "default" branch.

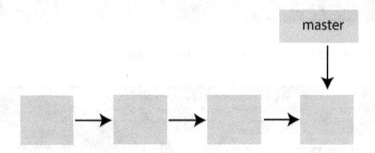

In most cases, the master is referred to as the main branch. Master branch is considered as the final view of the repo. Your local repository has its master branch that always up to date with the master of a remote repository.

Do not mess with the master. If you edited the master branch of a group project, your changes will affect everyone else and very quickly there will be merge conflicts.

Git Origin

In Git, The term origin is referred to the remote repository where you want to publish your commits. The default remote repository is called origin, although you can work with several remotes having a different name at the same time. It is said as an alias of the system.

Central Repository

Origin   Local Repository

The origin is a short name for the remote repository that a project was initially being cloned. It is used in place of the original repository URL. Thus, it makes referencing much easier.

Origin is just a standard convention. Although it is significant to leave this convention untouched, you could ideally rename it without losing any functionality.

In the following example, the URL parameter acts as an origin to the "clone" command for the cloned local repository:

```
$ git clone https://github.com/ImDwivedi1/Git-Example
```

Some commands in which the term origin and master are widely used are as follows:

❖ Git push origin master
❖ Git pull origin master

Git has two types of branches called local and remote. To use git pull and git push, you have to tell your local branch that on which branch is going to operate. So, the term origin master is used to deal with a remote repository and master branch. The term push origin master is used to push the changes to the remote repository. The term pull origin master is used to access the repository from remote to local.

Git Remote

In Git, the term remote is concerned with the remote repository. It is a shared repository that all team members use to exchange their changes. A remote repository is stored on a code hosting service like an internal server, GitHub, Subversion, and more. In the case of a local repository, a remote typically does not provide a file tree of the project's current state; as an alternative, it only consists of the .git versioning data.

The developers can perform many operations with the remote server. These operations can be a clone, fetch, push, pull, and more. Consider the below image:

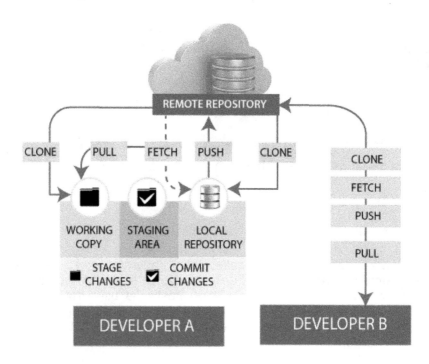

Check your Remote

To check the configuration of the remote server, run the git remote command. The git remote command allows accessing the connection between remote and local. If you want to see the original existence of your cloned repository, use the git remote command. It can be used as:

Syntax:

```
$ git remote
```

Output:

```
HiMaNshU@HiMaNshU-PC MINGW64 ~/Desktop/GitExample2 (master)
$ git remote
origin
```

The given command is providing the remote name as the origin. Origin is the default name for the remote server, which is given by Git.

Git remote -v:

Git remote supports a specific option -v to show the URLs that Git has stored as a short name. These short names are used during the reading and write operation. Here, -v stands for verbose. We can use --verbose in place of -v. It is used as:

Syntax:

```
$ git remote -v
```

Or

```
$ git remote --verbose
```

Output:

```
HiMaNshU@HiMaNshU-PC MINGW64 ~/Desktop/GitExample2 (master)
$ git remote -v
origin  https://github.com/ImDwivedi1/GitExample2.git (fetch)
origin  https://github.com/ImDwivedi1/GitExample2.git (push)
```

The above output is providing available remote connections. If a repository contains more than one remote connection, this command will list them all.

Git Remote Add

When we fetch a repository implicitly, git adds a remote for the repository. Also, we can explicitly add a remote for a repository. We can add a remote as a shot nickname or short name. To add remote as a short name, follow the below command:

Syntax:

```
$ git remote add <short name><remote URL>
```

Output:

```
HiMaNshU@HiMaNshU-PC MINGW64 ~/Desktop/Demo (master)
$ git remote add hd https://github.com/ImDwivedi1/hello-world

HiMaNshU@HiMaNshU-PC MINGW64 ~/Desktop/Demo (master)
$ git remote -v
hd      https://github.com/ImDwivedi1/hello-world (fetch)
hd      https://github.com/ImDwivedi1/hello-world (push)

HiMaNshU@HiMaNshU-PC MINGW64 ~/Desktop/Demo (master)
$
```

In the above output, I have added a remote repository with an existing repository as a short name "hd". Now, you can use "hd" on the command line in place of the whole URL. For example, you want to pull the repository, consider below output:

```
HiMaNshU@HiMaNshU-PC MINGW64 ~/Desktop/Demo (master)
$ git pull hd
warning: no common commits
remote: Enumerating objects: 12, done.
remote: Counting objects: 100% (12/12), done.
remote: Compressing objects: 100% (7/7), done.
remote: Total 12 (delta 2), reused 0 (delta 0), pack-reused 0
Unpacking objects: 100% (12/12), done.
From https://github.com/ImDwivedi1/hello-world
 * [new branch]      master      -> hd/master
You asked to pull from the remote 'hd', but did not specify
a branch. Because this is not the default configured remote
for your current branch, you must specify a branch on the command line
.
```

I have pulled a repository using its short name instead of its remote URL. Now, the repository master branch can be accessed through a short name.

Fetching and Pulling Remote Branch

You can fetch and pull data from the remote repository. The fetch and pull command goes out to that remote server, and fetch all the data from that remote project that you don't have yet. These commands let us fetch the references to all the branches from that remote.

To fetch the data from your remote projects, run the below command:

```
$ git fetch <remote>
```

To clone the remote repository from your remote projects, run the below command:

```
$ git clone<remote>
```

When we clone a repository, the remote repository is added by a default name "origin." So, mostly, the command is used as git fetch origin.

The git fetch origin fetches the updates that have been made to the remote server since you cloned it. The git fetch command only downloads the data to the local repository; it doesn't merge or modify the data until you don't operate. You have to merge it manually into your repository when you want.

To pull the repository, run the below command:

```
$ git pull <remote>
```

The git pull command automatically fetches and then merges the remote data into your current branch. Pulling is an easier and comfortable workflow than fetching. Because the git clone command sets up your local master branch to track the remote master branch on the server you cloned.

Pushing to Remote Branch

If you want to share your project, you have to push it upstream. The git push command is used to share a project or send updates to the remote server. It is used as:

```
$ git push <remote><branch>
```

To update the main branch of the project, use the below command:

```
$ git push origin master
```

It is a special command-line utility that specifies the remote branch and directory. When you have multiple branches on a remote server, then this command assists you to specify your main branch and repository.

Generally, the term origin stands for the remote repository, and master is considered as the main branch. So, the entire statement "git push origin master" pushed the local content on the master branch of the remote location.

Git Remove Remote

You can remove a remote connection from a repository. To remove a connection, perform the git remote command with remove or rm option. It can be done as:

Syntax:

```
$ git remote rm <destination>
```

Or

```
$ git remote remove <destination>
```

Consider the below example:

Suppose you are connected with a default remote server "origin." To check the remote verbosely, perform the below command:

```
$ git remote -v
```

Output:

```
HiMaNshU@HiMaNshU-PC MINGW64 ~/Desktop/GitExample2 (master)
$ git remote -v
origin  https://github.com/ImDwivedi1/GitExample2.git (fetch)
origin  https://github.com/ImDwivedi1/GitExample2.git (push)
```

The above output will list the available remote server. Now, perform the remove operation as mentioned above. Consider the below output:

```
HiMaNshU@HiMaNshU-PC MINGW64 ~/Desktop/GitExample2 (master)
$ git remote rm origin

HiMaNshU@HiMaNshU-PC MINGW64 ~/Desktop/GitExample2 (master)
$ git remote -v

HiMaNshU@HiMaNshU-PC MINGW64 ~/Desktop/GitExample2 (master)
$
```

In the above output, I have removed remote server "origin" from my repository.

Git Remote Rename

Git allows renaming the remote server name so that you can use a short name in place of the remote server name. Below command is used to rename the remote server:

Syntax:

```
$ git remote rename <old name><new name>
```

Output:

```
HiMaNshU@HiMaNshU-PC MINGW64 ~/Desktop/GitExample2 (master)
$ git remote rename origin hd

HiMaNshU@HiMaNshU-PC MINGW64 ~/Desktop/GitExample2 (master)
$ git remote -v
hd      https://github.com/ImDwivedi1/GitExample2 (fetch)
hd      https://github.com/ImDwivedi1/GitExample2 (push)
```

In the above output, I have renamed my default server name origin to hd. Now, I can operate using this name in place of origin. Consider the following output:

```
HiMaNshU@HiMaNshU-PC MINGW64 ~/Desktop/GitExample2 (master)
$ git pull hd master
From https://github.com/ImDwivedi1/GitExample2
 * branch              master      -> FETCH_HEAD
 * [new branch]        master      -> hd/master
Already up to date.

HiMaNshU@HiMaNshU-PC MINGW64 ~/Desktop/GitExample2 (master)
$ git pull origin  master
fatal: 'origin' does not appear to be a git repository
fatal: Could not read from remote repository.

Please make sure you have the correct access rights
and the repository exists.
```

In the above output, I have pulled the remote repository using the server name hd. But, when I am using the old server name, it is throwing an error with the message "'origin' does not appear to be a git repository." It means Git is not identifying the old name, so all the operations will be performed by a new name.

Git Show Remote

To see additional information about a particular remote, use the git remote command along with show sub-command. It is used as:

Syntax:

```
$ git remote show <remote>
```

It will result in information about the remote server. It contains a list of branches related to the remote and also the endpoints attached for fetching and pushing.

Output:

```
HiMaNshU@HiMaNshU-PC MINGW64 ~/Desktop/GitExample2 (master)
$ git remote show origin
* remote origin
  Fetch URL: https://github.com/ImDwivedi1/GitExample2
  Push  URL: https://github.com/ImDwivedi1/GitExample2
  HEAD branch: master
  Remote branches:
    BranchCherry    new (next fetch will store in remotes/orig
in)
    PullRequestDemo new (next fetch will store in remotes/orig
in)
    master          tracked
  Local ref configured for 'git push':
    master pushes to master (up to date)
```

The above output is listing the URLs for the remote repository as well as the tracking branch information. This information will be helpful in various cases.

Git Change Remote (Changing a Remote's URL)

We can change the URL of a remote repository. The git remote set command is used to change the URL of the repository. It changes an existing remote repository URL.

Git Remote Set:

We can change the remote URL simply by using the git remote set command. Suppose we want to make a unique name for our project to specify it. Git allows us to do so. It is a simple process. To change the remote URL, use the below command:

```
$ git remote set-url <remote name><newURL>
```

The remote set-url command takes two types of arguments. The first one is <remote name >, it is your current server name for the repository. The second argument is <newURL>, it is your new URL name for the repository. The <new URL> should be in below format: https://github.com/URLChanged

Consider the below image:

```
HiMaNshU@HiMaNshU-PC MINGW64 ~/Desktop/GitExample2 (master)
$ git remote set-url origin  https://github.com/URLChanged

HiMaNshU@HiMaNshU-PC MINGW64 ~/Desktop/GitExample2 (master)
$ git remote -v
origin  https://github.com/URLChanged (fetch)
origin  https://github.com/URLChanged (push)

HiMaNshU@HiMaNshU-PC MINGW64 ~/Desktop/GitExample2 (master)
$
```

In the above output, I have changed my existing repository URL as https://github.com/URLChanged from https://github.com/ImDwive di1/GitExample2. It can be understood by my URL name that I have changed this. To check the latest URL, perform the below command:

```
$ git remote -v
```

Branching & Merging

Git Branch

A branch is a version of the repository that diverges from the main working project. It is a feature available in most modern version control systems. A Git project can have more than one branch. These branches are a pointer to a snapshot of your changes. When you want to add a new feature or fix a bug, you spawn a new branch to summarize your changes. So, it is complex to merge the unstable code with the main code base and also facilitates you to clean up your future history before merging with the main branch.

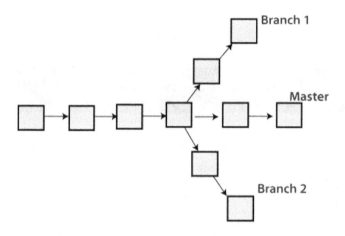

Git Master Branch

The master branch is a default branch in Git. It is instantiated when first commit made on the project. When you make the first commit, you're given a master branch to the starting commit point. When you start making a commit, then master branch pointer automatically moves forward. A repository can have only one master branch.

Master branch is the branch in which all the changes eventually get merged back. It can be called as an official working version of your project.

Operations on Branches

We can perform various operations on Git branches. The git branch command allows you to create, list, rename and delete branches. Many operations on branches are applied by git checkout and git merge command. So, the git branch is tightly integrated with the git checkout and git merge commands.

The Operations that can be performed on a branch:

Create Branch

You can create a new branch with the help of the git branch command. This command will be used as:

Syntax:

```
$ git branch  <branch name>
```

Output:

```
HiMaNshU@HiMaNshU-PC MINGW64 ~/Desktop/GitExample2 (master)
$ git branch B1
```

This command will create the branch B1 locally in Git directory.

List Branch

You can List all of the available branches in your repository by using the following command.

Either we can use git branch - list or git branch command to list the available branches in the repository.

Syntax:

```
$ git branch --list
```

or

```
$ git branch
```

Output:

```
HiMaNshU@HiMaNshU-PC MINGW64 ~/Desktop/GitExample2 (master)
$ git branch
  B1
  branch3
* master

HiMaNshU@HiMaNshU-PC MINGW64 ~/Desktop/GitExample2 (master)
$ git branch --list
  B1
  branch3
* master
```

Here, both commands are listing the available branches in the repository. The symbol * is representing currently active branch.

Delete Branch

You can delete the specified branch. It is a safe operation. In this command, Git prevents you from deleting the branch if it has unmerged changes. Below is the command to do this.

Syntax:

```
$ git branch -d<branch name>
```

Output:

```
HiMaNshU@HiMaNshU-PC MINGW64 ~/Desktop/GitExample2 (master)
$ git branch -d B1
Deleted branch B1 (was 554a122).
```

This command will delete the existing branch B1 from the repository.

The git branch d command can be used in two formats. Another format of this command is git branch D. The 'git branch D' command is used to delete the specified branch.

```
$ git branch -D <branch name>
```

Delete a Remote Branch

You can delete a remote branch from Git desktop application. Below command is used to delete a remote branch:

Syntax:

```
$ git push origin -delete <branch name>
```

```
HiMaNshU@HiMaNshU-PC MINGW64 ~/Desktop/GitExample2 (master)
$ git push origin --delete branch2
To https://github.com/ImDwivedi1/GitExample2
 - [deleted]          branch2

HiMaNshU@HiMaNshU-PC MINGW64 ~/Desktop/GitExample2 (master)
$
```

As you can see in the above output, the remote branch named branch2 from my GitHub account is deleted.

Switch Branch

Git allows you to switch between the branches without making a commit. You can switch between two branches with the git checkout command. To switch between the branches, below command is used:

```
$ git checkout<branch name>
```

Switch from master Branch

You can switch from master to any other branch available on your repository without making any commit.

Syntax:

```
$ git checkout <branch name>
```

Output:

```
HiMaNshU@HiMaNshU-PC MINGW64 ~/Desktop/GitExample2 (master)
$ git checkout branch4
Switched to branch 'branch4'
```

As you can see in the output, branches are switched from master to branch4 without making any commit.

Switch to master branch

You can switch to the master branch from any other branch with the help of below command.

Syntax:

```
$ git branch -m master
```

Output:

```
HiMaNshU@HiMaNshU-PC MINGW64 ~/Desktop/GitExample2 (branch4)
$ git checkout master
Switched to branch 'master'
Your branch is ahead of 'origin/master' by 1 commit.
  (use "git push" to publish your local commits)

HiMaNshU@HiMaNshU-PC MINGW64 ~/Desktop/GitExample2 (master)
$ |
```

As you can see in the above output, branches are switched from branch1 to master without making any commit.

Rename Branch

We can rename the branch with the help of the git branch command. To rename a branch, use the below command:

Syntax:

```
$ git branch -m <old branch name><new branch name>
```

Output:

```
HiMaNshU@HiMaNshU-PC MINGW64 ~/Desktop/GitExample2 (master)
$ git branch -m branch4 renamedB1

HiMaNshU@HiMaNshU-PC MINGW64 ~/Desktop/GitExample2 (master)
$ git branch
* master
  renamedB1

HiMaNshU@HiMaNshU-PC MINGW64 ~/Desktop/GitExample2 (master)
$ |
```

As you can see in the above output, branch4 renamed as renamedB1.

Merge Branch

Git allows you to merge the other branch with the currently active branch. You can merge two branches with the help of git merge command. Below command is used to merge the branches:

Syntax:

```
$ git merge <branch name>
```

Output:

```
HiMaNshU@HiMaNshU-PC MINGW64 ~/Desktop/GitExample2 (master)
$ git merge renamedB1
Already up to date.

HiMaNshU@HiMaNshU-PC MINGW64 ~/Desktop/GitExample2 (master)
$
```

From the above output, you can see that the master branch merged with renamedB1. Since I have made no-commit before merging, so the output is showing as already up to date.

Git Merge and Merge Conflict

In Git, the merging is a procedure to connect the forked history. It joins two or more development history together. The git merge command facilitates you to take the data created by git branch and integrate them into a single branch. Git merge will associate a series of commits into one unified history. Generally, git merge is used to combine two branches.

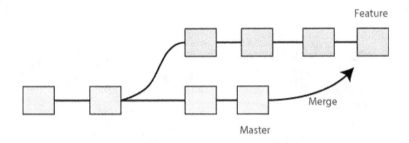

It is used to maintain distinct lines of development; at some stage, you want to merge the changes in one branch. It is essential to understand how merging works in Git.

In the above figure, there are two branches master and feature. We can see that we made some commits in both functionality and master branch, and merge them. It works as a pointer. It will find a common base commit between branches. Once Git finds a shared base commit, it will create a new "merge commit." It combines the changes of each queued merge commit sequence.

The "git merge" command
The git merge command is used to merge the branches.

The syntax for the git merge command is as:

```
$ git merge <query>
```

It can be used in various context. Some are as follows:

Scenario1: To merge the specified commit to currently active branch:

Use the below command to merge the specified commit to currently active branch.

```
$ git merge <commit>
```

The above command will merge the specified commit to the currently active branch. You can also merge the specified commit to a specified branch by passing in the branch name in <commit>. Let's see how to commit to a currently active branch.

See the below example. I have made some changes in my project's file newfile1.txt and committed it in my test branch.

```
HiMaNshU@HiMaNshU-PC MINGW64 ~/Desktop/GitExample2 (test)
$ git add newfile1.txt

HiMaNshU@HiMaNshU-PC MINGW64 ~/Desktop/GitExample2 (test)
$ git commit -m "edited newfile1.txt"
[test d2bb07d] edited newfile1.txt
 1 file changed, 1 insertion(+), 1 deletion(-)

HiMaNshU@HiMaNshU-PC MINGW64 ~/Desktop/GitExample2 (test)
$ git log
commit d2bb07dc9352e194b13075dcfd28e4de802c070b (HEAD -> test)
Author: ImDwivedi1 <himanshudubey481@gmail.com>
Date:   Wed Sep 25 11:27:44 2019 +0530

    edited newfile1.txt

commit 2852e020909dfe705707695fd6d715cd723f9540 (test2, master)
Author: ImDwivedi1 <himanshudubey481@gmail.com>
Date:   Wed Sep 25 10:29:07 2019 +0530

    newfile1 added
```

Copy the particular commit you want to merge on an active branch and perform the merge operation. See the following output:

```
HiMaNshU@HiMaNshU-PC MINGW64 ~/Desktop/GitExample2 (test)
$ git checkout test2
Switched to branch 'test2'

HiMaNshU@HiMaNshU-PC MINGW64 ~/Desktop/GitExample2 (test2)
$ git merge  d2bb07dc9352e194b13075dcfd28e4de802c070b
Updating 2852e02..d2bb07d
Fast-forward
 newfile1.txt | 2 +-
 1 file changed, 1 insertion(+), 1 deletion(-)

HiMaNshU@HiMaNshU-PC MINGW64 ~/Desktop/GitExample2 (test2)
$
```

In the above output, we have merged the previous commit in the active branch test2.

Scenario2: To merge commits into the master branch:

To merge a specified commit into master, first discover its commit id. Use the log command to find the particular commit id.

$git log

See the below output:

```
HiMaNshU@HiMaNshU-PC MINGW64 ~/Desktop/GitExample2 (test)
$ git log
commit 2852e020909dfe705707695fd6d715cd723f9540 (HEAD -> test)
Author: ImDwivedi1 <himanshudubey481@gmail.com>
Date:   Wed Sep 25 10:29:07 2019 +0530

    newfile1 added

commit 4a6693a71151323623c04dd75cb0d44c1c4dbadf (origin/master, origin/HEAD, mas
ter)
Merge: 30193f3 78c5fbd
Author: ImDwivedi1 <52317024+ImDwivedi1@users.noreply.github.com>
Date:   Mon Sep 9 15:24:13 2019 +0530

    Merge pull request #1 from ImDwivedi1/branch2

    Create merge the branch
```

To merge the commits into the master branch, switch over to the master branch.

$ git checkout master

Now, Switch to branch 'master' to perform merging operation on a commit. Use the git merge command along with master branch name. The syntax for this is as follows:

```
$ git merge master
```

See the below output:

```
HiMaNshU@HiMaNshU-PC MINGW64 ~/Desktop/GitExample2 (test)
$ git checkout master
Switched to branch 'master'
Your branch is up to date with 'origin/master'.

HiMaNshU@HiMaNshU-PC MINGW64 ~/Desktop/GitExample2 (master)
$ git merge 2852e020909dfe705707695fd6d715cd723f9540
Updating 4a6693a..2852e02
Fast-forward
 newfile.txt  | 1 +
 newfile1.txt | 1 +
 2 files changed, 2 insertions(+)
 create mode 100644 newfile.txt
 create mode 100644 newfile1.txt

HiMaNshU@HiMaNshU-PC MINGW64 ~/Desktop/GitExample2 (master)
$
```

As shown in the above output, the commit for the commit id *2852e020909dfe705707695fd6d715cd723f9540* has merged into the master branch. Two files have changed in master branch. However, we have made this commit in the test branch. So, it is possible to merge any commit in any of the branches.

Open new files, and you will notice that the new line that we have committed to the test branch is now copied on the master branch.

Scenario 3: Git merge branch.

Git allows merging the whole branch in another branch. Suppose you have made many changes on a branch and want to merge all of that at a time. Git allows you to do so. See the below example:

```
HiMaNshU@HiMaNshU-PC MINGW64 ~/Desktop/GitExample2 (test2)
$ git add newfile1.txt
```

In the given output, I have made changes in newfile1 on the test branch. Now, I have committed this change in the test branch.

```
HiMaNshU@HiMaNshU-PC MINGW64 ~/Desktop/GitExample2 (test2)
$ git commit -m "edit newfile1"
[test2 a3644e1] edit newfile1
 1 file changed, 1 insertion(+)
```

Now, switch to the desired branch you want to merge. In the given example, I have switched to the master branch. Perform the below command to merge the whole branch in the active branch.

```
$ git merge <branchname>
```

```
HiMaNshU@HiMaNshU-PC MINGW64 ~/Desktop/GitExample2 (test)
$ git checkout master
Switched to branch 'master'
Your branch is ahead of 'origin/master' by 1 commit.
  (use "git push" to publish your local commits)

HiMaNshU@HiMaNshU-PC MINGW64 ~/Desktop/GitExample2 (master)
$ git merge test2
Updating 2852e02..a3644e1
Fast-forward
 newfile1.txt | 3 ++-
 1 file changed, 2 insertions(+), 1 deletion(-)

HiMaNshU@HiMaNshU-PC MINGW64 ~/Desktop/GitExample2 (master)
$
```

As you can see from the given output, the whole commits of branch test2 have merged to branch master.

Git Merge Conflict

When two branches are trying to merge, and both are edited at the same time and in the same file, Git won't be able to identify which version is to take for changes. Such a situation is called merge conflict. If such a situation occurs, it stops just before the merge commit so that you can resolve the conflicts manually.

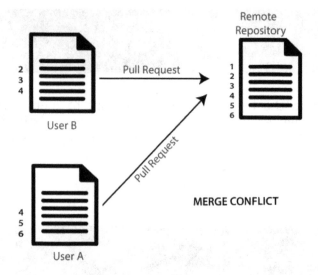

Let's understand it by an example.

Suppose my remote repository has cloned by two of my team member user1 and user2. The user1 made changes as below in my projects index file.

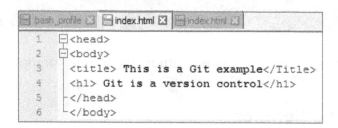

Update it in the local repository with the help of git add command.

```
HiMaNshU@HiMaNshU-PC MINGW64 ~/Desktop/user1repo (master)
$ git add index.html
```

Now commit the changes and update it with the remote repository. See the following output:

```
HiMaNshU@HiMaNshU-PC MINGW64 ~/Desktop/user1repo (master)
$ git commit -m "edited by user1"
[master fe4ef27] edited by user1
 1 file changed, 1 insertion(+)

HiMaNshU@HiMaNshU-PC MINGW64 ~/Desktop/user1repo (master)
$ git push origin master
Enumerating objects: 5, done.
Counting objects: 100% (5/5), done.
Delta compression using up to 2 threads
Compressing objects: 100% (3/3), done.
Writing objects: 100% (3/3), 345 bytes | 345.00 KiB/s, done.
Total 3 (delta 1), reused 0 (delta 0)
remote: Resolving deltas: 100% (1/1), completed with 1 local object.
To https://github.com/ImDwivedi1/Git-Example
   039c01b..fe4ef27  master -> master

HiMaNshU@HiMaNshU-PC MINGW64 ~/Desktop/user1repo (master)
```

Now, my remote repository will look like this:

It will show the status of the file like edited by whom and when.

Now, at the same time, user2 also update the index file as follows.

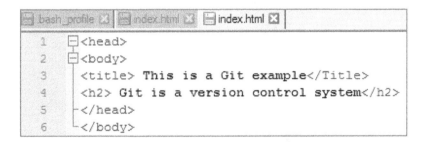

User2 has added and committed the changes in the local repository. But when he tries to push it to remote server, it will throw errors. See the following output:

```
HiMaNshU@HiMaNshU-PC MINGW64 ~/Desktop/user2repo (master)
$ git add index.html

HiMaNshU@HiMaNshU-PC MINGW64 ~/Desktop/user2repo (master)
$ git commit -m " edited by user2"
[master 3ee71e0]  edited by user2
 1 file changed, 1 insertion(+)

HiMaNshU@HiMaNshU-PC MINGW64 ~/Desktop/user2repo (master)
$ git push origin master
To https://github.com/ImDwivedi1/Git-Example
 ! [rejected]         master -> master (fetch first)
error: failed to push some refs to 'https://github.com/ImDwivedi1/Git-Example'
hint: Updates were rejected because the remote contains work that you do
hint: not have locally. This is usually caused by another repository pushing
hint: to the same ref. You may want to first integrate the remote changes
hint: (e.g., 'git pull ...') before pushing again.
hint: See the 'Note about fast-forwards' in 'git push --help' for details.

HiMaNshU@HiMaNshU-PC MINGW64 ~/Desktop/user2repo (master)
$
```

In the above output, the server knows that the file is already updated and not merged with other branches. So, the push request was rejected by the remote server. It will throw an error message like [rejected] failed to push some refs to <remote URL>. It will suggest you to pull the repository first before the push. See the below command:

```
HiMaNshU@HiMaNshU-PC MINGW64 ~/Desktop/user2repo (master)
$ git pull --rebase origin master
remote: Enumerating objects: 5, done.
remote: Counting objects: 100% (5/5), done.
remote: Compressing objects: 100% (2/2), done.
remote: Total 3 (delta 1), reused 3 (delta 1), pack-reused 0
Unpacking objects: 100% (3/3), done.
From https://github.com/ImDwivedi1/Git-Example
 * branch            master      -> FETCH_HEAD
   039c01b..fe4ef27  master      -> origin/master
First, rewinding head to replay your work on top of it...
Applying: edited by user2
Using index info to reconstruct a base tree...
M         index.html
Falling back to patching base and 3-way merge...
Auto-merging index.html
CONFLICT (content): Merge conflict in index.html
error: Failed to merge in the changes.
hint: Use 'git am --show-current-patch' to see the failed patch
Patch failed at 0001  edited by user2
Resolve all conflicts manually, mark them as resolved with
"git add/rm <conflicted_files>", then run "git rebase --continue".
You can instead skip this commit: run "git rebase --skip".
To abort and get back to the state before "git rebase", run "git rebase --abort"
.

HiMaNshU@HiMaNshU-PC MINGW64 ~/Desktop/user2repo (master|REBASE 1/1)
$
```

In the given output, git rebase command is used to pull the repository from the remote URL. Here, it will show the error message like merge conflict in <filename>.

Resolve Conflict:

To resolve the conflict, it is necessary to know whether the conflict occurs and why it occurs. Git merge tool command is used to resolve the conflict. The merge command is used as follows:

```
$ git mergetool
```

In my repository, it will result in:

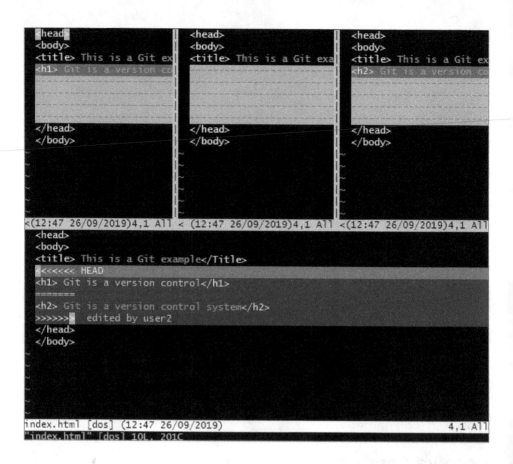

```
<head>                    <head>                    <head>
<body>                    <body>                    <body>
<title> This is a Git ex  <title> This is a Git exa  <title> This is a Git ex
<h1> Git is a version co                            <h2> Git is a version co




</head>                   </head>                   </head>
</body>                   </body>                   </body>



<(12:47 26/09/2019)4,1 All < (12:47 26/09/2019)4,1 All <(12:47 26/09/2019)4,1 All
<head>
<body>
<title> This is a Git example</Title>
<<<<<< HEAD
<h1> Git is a version control</h1>
=======
<h2> Git is a version control system</h2>
>>>>>>>    edited by user2
</head>
</body>




index.html [dos] (12:47 26/09/2019)                              4,1 All
"index.html" [dos] 10L. 201C
```

The above output shows the status of the conflicted file. To resolve the conflict, enter in the insert mode by merely pressing I key and make changes as you want. Press the Esc key, to come out from insert mode. Type the: w! at the bottom of the editor to save and exit the changes. To accept the changes, use the rebase command. It will be used as follows:

```
$ git rebase --continue
```

Hence, the conflict has resolved. See the below output:

```
HiMaNshU@HiMaNshU-PC MINGW64 ~/Desktop/user2repo (master|REBASE 1/1)
$ git rebase --continue
Applying:  edited by user2

HiMaNshU@HiMaNshU-PC MINGW64 ~/Desktop/user2repo (master)
$ git push origin master
Enumerating objects: 5, done.
Counting objects: 100% (5/5), done.
Delta compression using up to 2 threads
Compressing objects: 100% (3/3), done.
Writing objects: 100% (3/3), 373 bytes | 124.00 KiB/s, done.
Total 3 (delta 1), reused 0 (delta 0)
remote: Resolving deltas: 100% (1/1), completed with 1 local object.
To https://github.com/ImDwivedi1/Git-Example
   fe4ef27..b3db7dc  master -> master

HiMaNshU@HiMaNshU-PC MINGW64 ~/Desktop/user2repo (master)
$
```

In the above output, the conflict has resolved, and the local repository is synchronized with a remote repository.

To see that which is the first edited text of the merge conflict in your file, search the file attached with conflict marker <<<<<<<. You can see the changes from the HEAD or base branch after the line <<<<<<< HEAD in your text editor. Next, you can see the divider like =======. It divides your changes from the changes in the other branch, followed by >>>>>>> BRANCH-NAME. In the above example, user1 wrote "<h1> Git is a version control</h1>" in the base or HEAD branch and user2 wrote "<h2> Git is a version control</h2>".

Decide whether you want to keep only your branch's changes or the other branch's changes, or create a new change. Delete the conflict markers <<<<<<<, =======, >>>>>>> and create final changes you want to merge.

Git Rebase

Rebasing is a process to reapply commits on top of another base trip. It is used to apply a sequence of commits from distinct branches into a final commit. It is an alternative of git merge command. It is a linear process of merging.

In Git, the term rebase is referred to as the process of moving or combining a sequence of commits to a new base commit. Rebasing is very beneficial and it visualized the process in the environment of a feature branching workflow.

It is good to rebase your branch before merging it.

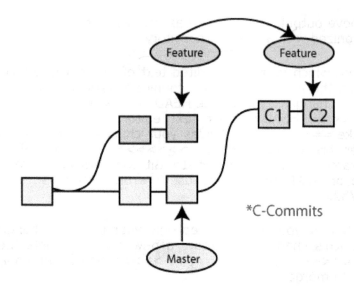

Generally, it is an alternative of git merge command. Merge is always a forward changing record. Comparatively, rebase is a compelling history rewriting tool in git. It merges the different commits one by one.

Suppose you have made three commits in your master branch and three in your other branch named test. If you merge this, then it will merge all commits in a time. But if you rebase it, then it will be merged in a linear manner. Consider the following image:

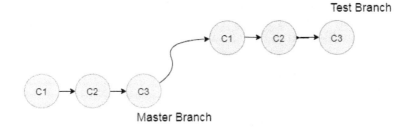

Test Branch

Master Branch

The above image describes how git rebase works. The three commits of the master branch are merged linearly with the commits of the test branch.

Merging is the most straightforward way to integrate the branches. It performs a three-way merge between the two latest branch commits.

How to Rebase

When you made some commits on a feature branch (test branch) and some in the master branch. You can rebase any of these branches. Use the git log command to track the changes (commit history). Checkout to the desired branch you want to rebase. Now perform the rebase command as follows:

Syntax:

```
$git rebase <branch name>
```

If there are some conflicts in the branch, resolve them, and perform below commands to continue changes:

```
$ git status
```

It is used to check the status,

```
$git rebase --continue
```

The above command is used to continue with the changes you made. If you want to skip the change, you can skip as follows:

```
$ git rebase --skip
```

When the rebasing is completed. Push the repository to the origin. Consider the below example to understand the git merge command.

Suppose that you have a branch say test2 on which you are working. You are now on the test2 branch and made some changes in the project's file newfile1.txt.

Add this file to repository:

```
$ git add newfile1.txt
```
Now, commit the changes. Use the below command:

```
$ git commit -m "new commit for test2 branch."
```
The output will look like:

```
[test2 a835504] new commitfor test2 branch
 1 file changed, 1 insertion(+)
```
Switch the branch to master:

```
$ git checkout master
```
Output:

```
Switched to branch 'master.'
Your branch is up to date with 'origin/master.'
```
Now you are on the master branch. I have added the changes to my file, says newfile.txt. The below command is used to add the file in the repository.

```
$ git add newfile.txt
```
Now commit the file for changes:

```
$ git commit -m " new commit made on the master branch."
```
Output:

```
[master 7fe5e7a]  new commit made on master
 1 file changed, 1 insertion(+)
HiMaNshU@HiMaNshU-PC MINGW64 ~/Desktop/GitExample2 (master)
```
To check the log history, perform the below command.

```
$ git log --oneline
```
Output:

```
HiMaNshU@HiMaNshU-PC MINGW64 ~/Desktop/GitExample2 (test)
$ git log --oneline
dfb5364 (HEAD -> test) commit2
4fddabb commit1
a3644e1 edit newfile1
d2bb07d edited newfile1.txt
2852e02 newfile1 added
4a6693a Merge pull request #1 from ImDwivedi1/branch2
30193f3 new files via upload
78c5fbd Create merge the branch
1d2bc03 Initial commit

HiMaNshU@HiMaNshU-PC MINGW64 ~/Desktop/GitExample2 (test)
$
```

As we can see in the log history, there is a new commit in the master branch. If I want to rebase my test2 branch, what should I do? See the below rebase branch scenario:

Rebase Branch

If we have many commits from distinct branches and want to merge it in one. To do so, we have two choices either we can merge it or rebase it. It is good to rebase your branch.

From the above example, we have committed to the master branch and want to rebase it on the test2 branch. Let's see the below commands:

$ git checkout test2

This command will switch you on the test2 branch from the master.

Output:

Switched to branch 'test2.'

Now you are on the test2 branch. Hence, you can rebase the test2 branch with the master branch. See the below command:

$ git rebase master

This command will rebase the test2 branch and will show as Applying: new commit on test2 branch. Consider the below output:

Output:

```
HiMaNshU@HiMaNshU-PC MINGW64 ~/Desktop/GitExample2 (test)
$ git rebase master
First, rewinding head to replay your work on top of it...
Fast-forwarded test to master.

HiMaNshU@HiMaNshU-PC MINGW64 ~/Desktop/GitExample2 (test)
$
```

Git Interactive Rebase

Git facilitates with Interactive Rebase; it is a potent tool that allows various operations like edit, rewrite, reorder, and more on existing commits. Interactive Rebase can only be operated on the currently checked out branch. Therefore, set your local HEAD branch at the sidebar.

Git interactive rebase can be invoked with rebase command, just type -i along with rebase command. Here 'i' stands for interactive. Syntax of this command is given below:

Syntax:

```
$ git rebase -i
```

It will list all the available interactive options.

Output:

```
HiMaNshU@HiMaNshU-PC MINGW64 ~/Desktop/GitExample2 (master)
$ git rebase -i
hint: Waiting for your editor to close the file... |
```

After the given output, it will open an editor with available options. Consider the below output:

Output:

```
git-rebase-todo

  4  #
  5  # Commands:
  6  # p, pick <commit> = use commit
  7  # r, reword <commit> = use commit, but edit the commit message
  8  # e, edit <commit> = use commit, but stop for amending
  9  # s, squash <commit> = use commit, but meld into previous commit
 10  # f, fixup <commit> = like "squash", but discard this commit's log message
 11  # x, exec <command> = run command (the rest of the line) using shell
 12  # b, break = stop here (continue rebase later with 'git rebase --continue')
 13  # d, drop <commit> = remove commit
 14  # l, label <label> = label current HEAD with a name
 15  # t, reset <label> = reset HEAD to a label
 16  # m, merge [-C <commit> | -c <commit>] <label> [# <oneline>]
 17  # .        create a merge commit using the original merge commit's
 18  # .        message (or the oneline, if no original merge commit was
 19  # .        specified). Use -c <commit> to reword the commit message.
 20  #
 21  # These lines can be re-ordered; they are executed from top to bottom.
 22  #
 23  # If you remove a line here THAT COMMIT WILL BE LOST.
 24  #
 25  # However, if you remove everything, the rebase will be aborted.
 26  #
 27  # Note that empty commits are commented outp
 28
 29  # Rebase 0a1a475..0a1a475 onto 0a1a475 (1 command)
 30  #
 31  # Commands:
```

When we perform the git interactive rebase command, it will open your default text editor with the above output.

The options it contains are listed below:

- ❖ Pick
- ❖ Reword
- ❖ Edit
- ❖ Squash
- ❖ Fixup
- ❖ Exec
- ❖ Break
- ❖ Drop
- ❖ Label
- ❖ Reset
- ❖ Merge

The above options perform their specific tasks with git-rebase. Let's understand each of these options in brief.

Pick (-p):

Pick stands here that the commit is included. Order of the commits depends upon the order of the pick commands during rebase. If you do not want to add a commit, you have to delete the entire line.

Reword (-r):

The reword is quite similar to pick command. The reword option paused the rebase process and provides a chance to alter the commit message. It does not affect any changes made by the commit.

Edit (-e):

The edit option allows for amending the commit. The amending means, commits can be added or changed entirely. We can also make additional commits before rebase continue command. It allows us to split a large commit into the smaller commit; moreover, we can remove erroneous changes made in a commit.

Squash (-s):

The squash option allows you to combine two or more commits into a single commit. It also allows us to write a new commit message for describing the changes.

Fixup (-f):

It is quite similar to the squash command. It discarded the message of the commit to be merged. The older commit message is used to describe both changes.

Exec (-x):

The exec option allows you to run arbitrary shell commands against a commit.

Break (-b):

The break option stops the rebasing at just position. It will continue rebasing later with 'git rebase --continue' command.

Drop (-d):

The drop option is used to remove the commit.

Label (-l):

The label option is used to mark the current head position with a name.

Reset (-t):

The reset option is used to reset head to a label.

GitMerge vs. Rebase

It is a most common puzzling question for the git user's that when to use merge command and when to use rebase. Both commands are similar, and both are used to merge the commits made by the different branches of a repository.

Rebasing is not recommended in a shared branch because the rebasing process will create inconsistent repositories. For individuals, rebasing can be more useful than merging. If you want to see the complete history, you should use the merge. Merge tracks the entire history of commits, while rebase rewrites a new one.

Git rebase commands said as an alternative of git merge. However, they have some key differences:

Git Merge	Git Rebase
Merging creates a final commit at merging.	Git rebase does not create any commit at rebasing.
It merges all commits as a single commit.	It creates a linear track of commits.
It creates a graphical history that might be a bit complex to understand.	It creates a linear history that can be easily understood.
It is safe to merge two branches.	Git "rebase" deals with the severe operation.
Merging can be performed on both public and private branches.	It is the wrong choice to use rebasing on public branches.
Merging integrates the content of the feature branch with the master branch. So, the master branch is changed, and feature branch history remains consistence.	Rebasing of the master branch may affect the feature branch.
Merging preserves history.	Rebasing rewrites history.
Git merge presents all conflicts at once.	Git rebase presents conflicts one by one.

Git Squash

In Git, the term squash is used to squash the previous commits into one. It is not a command; instead, it is a keyword. The squash is an excellent technique for group-specific changes before forwarding them to others. You can merge several commits into a single commit with the compelling interactive rebase command.

If you are a Git user, then you must have realized the importance of squashing a commit. Especially if you are an open-source contributor, then many times, you have to create a PR (pull request) with squashed commit. You can also squash commits if you have already created a PR.

Let's understand how to squash commits?

Git Squash Commits

Being a responsible contributor to Git, it is necessary to make the collaboration process efficient and meaningful. Git allows some powerful collaboration tools in different ways. Git squash is one of the powerful tools that facilitate efficient and less painful collaboration.

The squash is not any command; instead, it's one of many options available to you under git interactive rebases. The squash allows us to rewrite history. Suppose we have made many commits during the project work, squashing all the commits into a large commit is the right choice than pushing. Let's understand how to squash two commits.

Step1: Check the commit history

To check the commit history, run the below command:

```
$ git log --oneline
```

The given command will display the history in one line. We can track the history and choose the commits we want to squash. Consider the following output:

```
HiMaNshU@HiMaNshU-PC MINGW64 ~/Desktop/GitExample2 (master)
$ git log --oneline
4512e2e (HEAD -> master) Removed another line from the reposito
aefc924 Removed last lione from the repository
0d3835a newfile2 Re-added
56afce0 (tag: -d, tag: --delete, tag: --d, tag: projectv1.1, or
d an empty newfile2
0d5191f added a new image to prject
828b962 (tag: olderversion) Update design2.css
0a1a475 (test) CSS file
f1ddc7c new comit on test2 branch
7fe5e7a  new commit in master branch
dfb5364 commit2
4fddabb commit1
a3644e1 edit newfile1
d2bb07d edited newfile1.txt
2852e02 newfile1 added
4a6693a Merge pull request #1 from ImDwivedi1/branch2
30193f3 new files via upload
78c5fbd Create merge the branch
1d2bc03 Initial commit
```

Step 2: Choose the commits to squash.

Suppose we want to squash the last commits. To squash commits, run the below command:

```
$ git rebase -i HEAD ~3
```

The above command will open your default text editor and will squash the last three commits. The editor will open as follows:

```
pick 0d3835a newfile2 Re-added
pick aefc924 Removed last lione from the repository
pick 4512e2e Removed another line from the repository

# Rebase 56afce0..4512e2e onto 56afce0 (3 commands)
#
# Commands:
# p, pick <commit> = use commit
# r, reword <commit> = use commit, but edit the commit message
# e, edit <commit> = use commit, but stop for amending
# s, squash <commit> = use commit, but meld into previous commi
t
# f, fixup <commit> = like "squash", but discard this commit's
log message
# x, exec <command> = run command (the rest of the line) using
shell
# b, break = stop here (continue rebase later with 'git rebase
--continue')
# d, drop <commit> = remove commit
# l, label <label> = label current HEAD with a name
# t, reset <label> = reset HEAD to a label
# m, merge [-C <commit> | -c <commit>] <label> [# <oneline>]
# .       create a merge commit using the original merge commit
's
# .       message (or the oneline, if no original merge commit
was
@@@
</rebase-merge/git-rebase-todo [unix] (16:43 14/11/2019)1,1 Top
<it/rebase-merge/git-rebase-todo" [unix] 29L, 1273C
```

From the above image, we can see previous commits shown at the top
of the editor. If we want to merge them into a single commit, then we
have to replace the word pick with the squash on the top of the editor.
To write on the editor, press 'i' button to enter in insert mode. After
editing the document, press the :wq to save and exit from the editor.

Step 3: update the commits

On pressing enter key, a new window of the text editor will be opened
to confirm the commit. We can edit the commit message on this
screen.

I am editing my first commit message because it will be a combination
of all three commits. Consider the below image:

```
# This is a combination of 3 commits.
# This is the 1st commit message:

newfile2 Re-added

# This is the commit message #2:

Removed last lione from the repository

# This is the commit message #3:

Removed another line from the repository

# Please enter the commit message for your changes. Lines start
ing
# with '#' will be ignored, and an empty message aborts the com
mit.
#
# Date:        Fri Nov 8 15:49:51 2019 +0530
#
# interactive rebase in progress; onto 56afce0
# Last commands done (3 commands done):
#    squash aefc924 Removed last lione from the repository
#    squash 4512e2e Removed another line from the repository
# No commands remaining.
# You are currently rebasing branch 'master' on '56afce0'.
#
<tExample2/.git/COMMIT_EDITMSG [unix] (16:44 14/11/2019)1,1 Top
</GitExample2/.git/COMMIT_EDITMSG" [unix] 30L, 826C
```

The above image is the editor screen to confirm the merging of commits. Here we can update the commit messages. To edit on this editor, press the 'i' button for insert mode and edit the desired text. Press the :wq keys, to save and exit from the editor.

When we exit the editor, it will show the description of updates. Consider the below output:

```
HiMaNshU@HiMaNshU-PC MINGW64 ~/Desktop/GitExample2 (master)
$ git rebase -i HEAD~3
[detached HEAD a3a4f45] Removed last lione from the repository
 Date: Fri Nov 8 15:49:51 2019 +0530
 3 files changed, 4 deletions(-)
 delete mode 100644 newfile.txt
 delete mode 100644 newfile2.txt
Successfully rebased and updated refs/heads/master.
```

The above output is listing the description of changes that have been made on the repository. Now, the commits have been squashed. Check the commit history for confirmation with the help of the git log. Consider the below output:

```
HiMaNShU@HiMaNShU-PC MINGW64 ~/Desktop/GitExample2 (master)
$ git log --oneline
a3a4f45 (HEAD -> master) Removed last lione from the repository
56afce0 (tag: -d, tag: --delete, tag: --d, tag: projectv1.1, or
igin/master, testing) Added an empty newfile2
0d5191f added a new image to prject
828b962 (tag: olderversion) Update design2.css
0a1a475 (test) CSS file
f1ddc7c new comit on test2 branch
7fe5e7a  new commit in master branch
dfb5364 commit2
4fddabb commit1
a3644e1 edit newfile1
d2bb07d edited newfile1.txt
2852e02 newfile1 added
4a6693a Merge pull request #1 from ImDwivedi1/branch2
30193f3 new files via upload
78c5fbd Create merge the branch
1d2bc03 Initial commit
```

Step 4: Push the squashed commit

Now, we can push this squashed commit on the remote server. To push this squashed commit, run the below command:

```
$ git push origin master
```

Or

```
$ git push -f origin master
```

The above command will push the changes on the remote server. We can check this commit on our remote repository. Consider the below image:

ImDwivedi1 Removed last lione from the repository ...	
README.md	Initial commit
abc.jpg	added a new image to prject
design.css	new files via upload
design2.css	Update design2.css
index.jsp	new files via upload
master.jsp	new files via upload
merge the branch	Create merge the branch
newfile1.txt	Removed last lione from the repository

As you can see from the above image. A new commit has been added to my remote repository.

Drawbacks of Squashing

There are no significant drawbacks of squashing. But we can consider some facts that may affect the project. These facts are as follows:

The squashing commits, and rebasing changes the history of the repository. If any contributor does not pay attention to the updated history, then it may create conflict. I suggest a clean history because it is more valuable than another one. Although we can check the original history in the ref log.

There is another drawback, we may lose granularity because of squashing. Try to make minimum squashes while working with Git. So, if you are new on Git, then try to stay away from squash.

Collaborating

Git Fetch

Git "fetch" Downloads commits, objects and refs from another repository. It fetches branches and tags from one or more repositories. It holds repositories along with the objects that are necessary to complete their histories to keep updated remote-tracking branches.

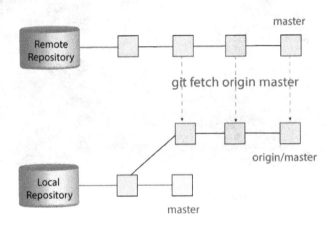

The "git fetch"command

The "git fetch" command is used to pull the updates from remote-tracking branches. Additionally, we can get the updates that have been pushed to our remote branches to our local machines. As we know, a branch is a variation of our repositories main code, so the remote-tracking branches are branches that have been set up to pull and push from remote repository.

How to fetch Git Repository

We can use fetch command with many arguments for a particular data fetch. See the following scenarios to understand the uses of fetch command.

Scenario 1: To fetch the remote repository:

We can fetch the complete repository with the help of fetch command from a repository URL like a pull command does. See the below output:

Syntax:

```
$ git fetch< repository Url>
```

Output:

```
HiMaNshU@HiMaNshU-PC MINGW64 ~/Desktop/Git-Example (master)
$ git fetch https://github.com/ImDwivedi1/Git-Example.git
warning: no common commits
remote: Enumerating objects: 6, done.
remote: Counting objects: 100% (6/6), done.
remote: Compressing objects: 100% (4/4), done.
remote: Total 6 (delta 0), reused 0 (delta 0), pack-reused 0
Unpacking objects: 100% (6/6), done.
From https://github.com/ImDwivedi1/Git-Example
 * branch            HEAD           -> FETCH_HEAD

HiMaNshU@HiMaNshU-PC MINGW64 ~/Desktop/Git-Example (master)
$ |
```

In the above output, the complete repository has fetched from a remote URL.

Scenario 2: To fetch a specific branch:

We can fetch a specific branch from a repository. It will only access the element from a specific branch. See the below output:

Syntax:

```
$ git fetch <branch URL><branch name>
```

Output:

```
HiMaNshU@HiMaNshU-PC MINGW64 ~/Desktop/Git-Example (master)
$ git fetch https://github.com/ImDwivedi1/Git-Example.git Test
warning: no common commits
remote: Enumerating objects: 9, done.
remote: Counting objects: 100% (9/9), done.
remote: Compressing objects: 100% (6/6), done.
remote: Total 9 (delta 1), reused 0 (delta 0), pack-reused 0
Unpacking objects: 100% (9/9), done.
From https://github.com/ImDwivedi1/Git-Example
 * branch             Test        -> FETCH_HEAD

HiMaNshU@HiMaNshU-PC MINGW64 ~/Desktop/Git-Example (master)
$ |
```

In the given output, the specific branch test has fetched from a remote URL.

Scenario 3: To fetch all the branches simultaneously:

The git fetch command allows to fetch all branches simultaneously from a remote repository. See the below example:

Syntax:

```
$ git fetch -all
```

Output:

```
HiMaNshU@HiMaNshU-PC MINGW64 ~/Desktop/Git-Example (master)
$ git fetch --all
Fetching origin
From https://github.com/ImDwivedi1/Git-Example
 * [new branch]      master      -> origin/master
 * [new branch]      Test        -> origin/Test

HiMaNshU@HiMaNshU-PC MINGW64 ~/Desktop/Git-Example (master)
$
```

In the above output, all the branches have fetched from the repository Git-Example.

Scenario 4: To synchronize the local repository:

Suppose, your team member has added some new features to your remote repository. So, to add these updates to your local repository, use the git fetch command. It is used as follows.

Syntax:

```
$ git fetch origin
```

Output:

```
HiMaNshU@HiMaNshU-PC MINGW64 ~/Desktop/Git-Example (master)
$ git fetch origin

HiMaNshU@HiMaNshU-PC MINGW64 ~/Desktop/Git-Example (master)
$ git fetch origin
remote: Enumerating objects: 4, done.
remote: Counting objects: 100% (4/4), done.
remote: Compressing objects: 100% (2/2), done.
remote: Total 3 (delta 1), reused 0 (delta 0), pack-reused 0
Unpacking objects: 100% (3/3), done.
From https://github.com/ImDwivedi1/Git-Example
 * [new branch]      test2       -> origin/test2

HiMaNshU@HiMaNshU-PC MINGW64 ~/Desktop/Git-Example (master)
$ |
```

In the above output, new features of the remote repository have updated to my local system. In this output, the branch test2 and its objects are added to the local repository.

The git fetch can fetch from either a single named repository or URL or from several repositories at once. It can be considered as the safe version of the git pull commands.

The git fetch downloads the remote content but not update your local repo's working state. When no remote server is specified, by default, it will fetch the origin remote.

Differences between git fetch and git pull

To understand the differences between fetch and pull, let's know the similarities between both of these commands. Both commands are used to download the data from a remote repository. But both of these commands work differently. Like when you do a git pull, it gets all the changes from the remote or central repository and makes it available to your corresponding branch in your local repository. When you do a git fetch, it fetches all the changes from the remote repository and stores it in a separate branch in your local repository. You can reflect those changes in your corresponding branches by merging.

So basically,

Git Fetch vs. Pull

Some of the key differences between both of these commands are as follows:

git fetch	git pull
Fetch downloads only new data from a remote repository.	Pull is used to update your current HEAD branch with the latest changes from the remote server.
Fetch is used to get a new view of all the things that happened in a remote repository.	Pull downloads new data and directly integrates it into your current working copy files.
Fetch never manipulates or spoils data.	Pull downloads the data and integrates it with the current working file.
It protects your code from merge conflict.	In git pull, there are more chances to create the merge conflict.
It is better to use git fetch command with git merge command on a pulled repository.	It is not an excellent choice to use git pull if you already pulled any repository.

Git Pull / Pull Request

The term pull is used to receive data from GitHub. It fetches and merges changes from the remote server to your working directory. The git pull command is used to pull a repository.

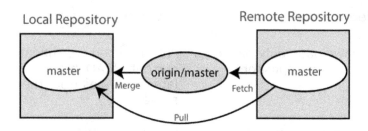

Pull request is a process for a developer to notify team members that they have completed a feature. Once their feature branch is ready, the developer files a pull request via their remote server account. Pull request announces all the team members that they need to review the code and merge it into the master branch.

The below figure demonstrates how pull acts between different locations and how it is similar or dissimilar to other related commands.

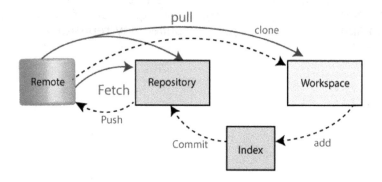

The "git pull" command

The pull command is used to access the changes (commits)from a remote repository to the local repository. It updates the local branches with the remote-tracking branches. Remote tracking branches are branches that have been set up to push and pull from the remote repository. Generally, it is a collection of the fetch and merges command. First, it fetches the changes from remote and combined them with the local repository.

The syntax of the git pull command is given below:

Syntax:

```
$ git pull <option> [<repository URL><refspec>...]
```

In which:

<option>: Options are the commands; these commands are used as an additional option in a particular command. Options can be -q (quiet), -v (verbose), -e(edit) and more.

<repository URL>: Repository URL is your remote repository's URL where you have stored your original repositories like GitHub or any other git service. This URL looks like:

```
https://github.com/ImDwivedi1/GitExample2.git
```

To access this URL, go to your account on GitHub and select the repository you want to clone. After that, click on the clone or download option from the repository menu. A new pop up window will open, select clone with https option from available options. See the below screenshot:

Copy the highlighted URL. This URL is used to Clone the repository.

<Refspec>: A ref is referred to commit, for example, head (branches), tags, and remote branches. You can check head, tags, and remote repository in .git/ref directory on your local repository. Refspec specifies and updates the refs.

How to use pull:

It is essential to understand how it works and how to use it. Let's take an example to understand how it works and how to use it. Suppose I have added a new file say design2.css in my remote repository of project GitExample2.

To create the file first, go to create a file option given on repository sub-functions. After that, select the file name and edit the file as you want. Consider the following image.

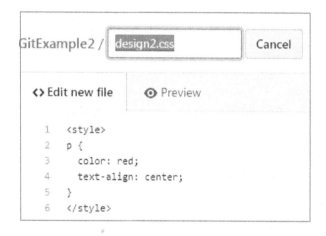

Go to the bottom of the page, select a commit message and description of the file. Select whether you want to create a new branch or commit it directly in the master branch. Consider the following image:

Commit new file

> CSS file

> See the proposed CSS file.

- ● ⊶ Commit directly to the `master` branch.
- ○ ⌥ Create a new branch for this commit and start a pull request. Learn more about pull requests.

Commit new file   Cancel

Now, we have successfully committed the changes.

To pull these changes in your local repository, perform the git pull operation on your cloned repository. There are many specific options available for pull command. Let's have a look at some of its usage.

Default git pull:

We can pull a remote repository by just using the git pull command. It's a default option. Syntax of git pull is given below:

Syntax:

```
$ git pull
```

Output:

```
HiMaNshU@HiMaNshU-PC MINGW64 ~/Desktop/GitExample2 (master)
$ git pull
remote: Enumerating objects: 4, done.
remote: Counting objects: 100% (4/4), done.
remote: Compressing objects: 100% (3/3), done.
remote: Total 3 (delta 1), reused 0 (delta 0), pack-reused 0
Unpacking objects: 100% (3/3), done.
From https://github.com/ImDwivedi1/GitExample2
   f1ddc7c..0a1a475  master      -> origin/master
Updating f1ddc7c..0a1a475
Fast-forward
 design2.css | 6 ++++++
 1 file changed, 6 insertions(+)
 create mode 100644 design2.css

HiMaNshU@HiMaNshU-PC MINGW64 ~/Desktop/GitExample2 (master)
$ |
```

In the given output, the newly updated objects of the repository are
fetched through the git pull command. It is the default version of the
git pull command. It will update the newly created file design2.css file
and related object in the local repository. See the below image.

Name	Date modified	Type	Size
.git	10/1/2019 2:47 PM	File folder	
newfolder3	9/21/2019 11:37 AM	File folder	
design	9/19/2019 6:10 PM	Cascading Style S...	1 KB
design2	10/1/2019 2:47 PM	Cascading Style S...	1 KB
index	9/19/2019 6:10 PM	JSP File	2 KB
master	9/19/2019 6:10 PM	JSP File	1 KB
merge the branch	9/20/2019 6:05 PM	File	1 KB
newfile	9/28/2019 12:56 PM	Text Document	1 KB
newfile1	9/28/2019 4:01 PM	Text Document	1 KB
README	9/19/2019 6:10 PM	MD File	1 KB

As you can see in the above output, the design2.css file is added to the
local repository. The git pull command is equivalent to git fetch origin
head and git merge head. The head is referred to as the ref of the
current branch.

Git Pull Remote Branch

Git allows fetching a particular branch. Fetching a remote branch is a
similar process, as mentioned above, in git pull command. The only
difference is we have to copy the URL of the particular branch we want
to pull. To do so, we will select a specific branch. See the below
image:

In the above screenshot, I have chosen my branch named edited to copy the URL of the edited branch. Now, I am going to pull the data from the edited branch. Below command is used to pull a remote branch:

Syntax:

```
$ git pull <remote branch URL>
```

Output:

```
HiMaNshU@HiMaNshU-PC MINGW64 ~/Desktop/Demo (master)
$ git pull https://github.com/ImDwivedi1/GitExample2.git
remote: Enumerating objects: 38, done.
remote: Counting objects: 100% (38/38), done.
remote: Compressing objects: 100% (25/25), done.
remote: Total 38 (delta 13), reused 19 (delta 7), pack-reused 0
Unpacking objects: 100% (38/38), done.
From https://github.com/ImDwivedi1/GitExample2
 * branch            HEAD       -> FETCH_HEAD

HiMaNshU@HiMaNshU-PC MINGW64 ~/Desktop/Demo (master)
$
```

In the above output, the remote branch edited has copied.

Git Force Pull

Git force pull allows for pulling your repository at any cost. Suppose the below scenario:

If you have updated any file locally and other team members updated it on the remote. So, when will you fetch the repository, it may create a conflict.

We can say force pull is used for overwriting the files. If we want to discard all the changes in the local repository, then we can overwrite it by influentially pulling it. Consider the below process to force pull a repository:

Step1: Use the git fetch command to download the latest updates from the remote without merging or rebasing.

```
$ git fetch -all
```

Step2: Use the git reset command to reset the master branch with updates that you fetched from remote. The hard option is used to forcefully change all the files in the local repository with a remote repository.

```
$ git reset -hard <remote>/<branch_name>
$ git reset-hard master
```

Consider the below output:

```
HiMaNshU@HiMaNshU-PC MINGW64 ~/Desktop/Demo/GitExample2 (master)
$ git fetch --all
Fetching origin
remote: Enumerating objects: 5, done.
remote: Counting objects: 100% (5/5), done.
remote: Compressing objects: 100% (3/3), done.
remote: Total 3 (delta 1), reused 0 (delta 0), pack-reused 0
Unpacking objects: 100% (3/3), done.
From https://github.com/ImDwivedi1/GitExample2
   0a1a475..828b962  master      -> origin/master

HiMaNshU@HiMaNshU-PC MINGW64 ~/Desktop/Demo/GitExample2 (master)
$ git reset --hard master
HEAD is now at 0a1a475 CSS file
```

In the above output, I have updated my design2.css file and forcefully pull it into the repository.

Git Pull Origin Master

There is another way to pull the repository. We can pull the repository by using the git pull command. The syntax is given below:

```
$ git pull <options><remote>/<branchname>
$ git pull origin master
```

In the above syntax, the term origin stands for the repository location where the remote repository situated. Master is considered as the main branch of the project.

Consider the below output:

```
HiMaNshU@HiMaNshU-PC MINGW64 ~/Desktop/Demo/GitExample2 (master)
$ git pull origin master
From https://github.com/ImDwivedi1/GitExample2
 * branch            master      -> FETCH_HEAD
Updating 0a1a475..828b962
Fast-forward
 design2.css | 1 +
 1 file changed, 1 insertion(+)

HiMaNshU@HiMaNshU-PC MINGW64 ~/Desktop/Demo/GitExample2 (master)
$
```

It will overwrite the existing data of the local repository with a remote repository.

You can check the remote location of your repository. To check the remote location of the repository, use the below command:

```
$ git remote -v
```

The given command will result in a remote location like this:

```
origin  https://github.com/ImDwivedi1/GitExample2 (fetch)
origin  https://github.com/ImDwivedi1/GitExample2 (push)
```

The output displays fetch and push both locations. Consider the below image:

```
HiMaNshU@HiMaNshU-PC MINGW64 ~/Desktop/Demo/GitExample2 (master)
$ git remote -v
origin  https://github.com/ImDwivedi1/GitExample2 (fetch)
origin  https://github.com/ImDwivedi1/GitExample2 (push)
```

Git Pull Request

Pull request allows you to announce a change made by you in the branch. Once a pull request is opened, you are allowed to converse and review the changes made by others. It allows reviewing commits before merging into the main branch.

Pull request is created when you committed a change in the GitHub project, and you want it to be reviewed by other members. You can commit the changes into a new branch or an existing branch.

Once you've created a pull request, you can push commits from your branch to add them to your existing pull request.

How to Create a Pull Request

To create a pull request, you need to create a file and commit it as a new branch. As we mentioned earlier in this topic, how to commit a file to use git pull. Select the option "create a new branch for this commit and start a pull request" from the bottom of the page. Give the name of the new branch. Select the option to propose a new file at the bottom of the page. Consider the below image.

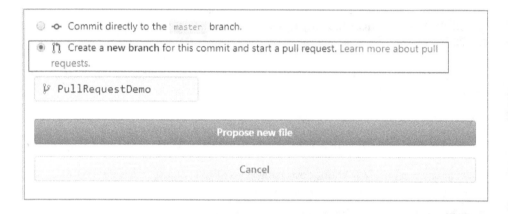

In the above image, I have selected the required option and named the file as PullRequestDemo. Select the option to propose a new file. It will open a new page. Select the option create pull request. Consider the below image:

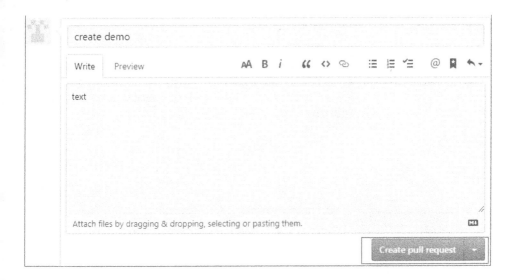

Now, the pull request is created by you. People can see this request. They can merge this request with the other branches by selecting a merged pull request.

Git Push

The push term refers to upload local repository content to a remote repository. Pushing is an act of transfer commits from your local repository to a remote repository. Pushing is capable of overwriting changes; caution should be taken when pushing.

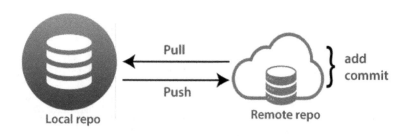

Moreover, we can say the push updates the remote refs with local refs. Every time you push into the repository, it is updated with some interesting changes that you made. If we do not specify the location of a repository, then it will push to default location at origin master.

The "git push" command is used to push into the repository. The push command can be considered as a tool to transfer commits between local and remote repositories. The basic syntax is given below:

```
$ git push <option> [<Remote URL><branch name><refspec>...]
```

Push command supports many additional options. Some options are as follows under push tags.

Git Push Tags

<repository>: The repository is the destination of a push operation. It can be either a URL or the name of a remote repository.

<refspec>: It specifies the destination ref to update source object.

--all: The word "all" stands for all branches. It pushes all branches.

--prune: It removes the remote branches that do not have a local counterpart. Means, if you have a remote branch say demo, if this branch does not exist locally, then it will be removed.

--mirror: It is used to mirror the repository to the remote. Updated or Newly created local refs will be pushed to the remote end. It can be force updated on the remote end. The deleted refs will be removed from the remote end.

--dry-run: Dry run tests the commands. It does all this except originally update the repository.

--tags: It pushes all local tags.

--delete: It deletes the specified branch.

-u: It creates an upstream tracking connection. It is very useful if you are going to push the branch for the first time.

Git Push Origin Master

Git push origin master is a special command-line utility that specifies the remote branch and directory. When you have multiple branches and directory, then this command assists you in determining your main branch and repository.

Generally, the term origin stands for the remote repository, and master is considered as the main branch. So, the entire statement "git push origin master" pushed the local content on the master branch of the remote location.

Syntax:

```
$ git push origin master
```

Let's understand this statement with an example.

Let's make a new commit to my existing repository, say GitExample2. I have added an image to my local repository named abc.jpg and committed the changes. Consider the following image:

```
HiMaNshU@HiMaNshU-PC MINGW64 ~/Desktop/GitExample2 (master)
$ git status
On branch master
Your branch is up to date with 'origin/master'.

Untracked files:
  (use "git add <file>..." to include in what will be committed)
        abc.jpg

nothing added to commit but untracked files present (use "git add" to trac

HiMaNshU@HiMaNshU-PC MINGW64 ~/Desktop/GitExample2 (master)
$ git add abc.jpg

HiMaNshU@HiMaNshU-PC MINGW64 ~/Desktop/GitExample2 (master)
$ git commit -m "added a new image to prject"
[master 0d5191f] added a new image to prject
 1 file changed, 0 insertions(+), 0 deletions(-)
 create mode 100644 abc.jpg
```

In the above output, I have attached a picture to my local repository. The git status command is used to check the status of the repository. The git status command will be performed as follows:

```
$ git status
```

It shows the status of the untracked image abc.jpg. Now, add the image and commit the changes as:

```
$ git add abc.jpg
```

$git commit -m "added a new image to project."

The image is wholly tracked in the local repository. Now, we can push it to origin master as:

```
$ git push origin master
```

Output:

```
HiMaNshU@HiMaNshU-PC MINGW64 ~/Desktop/GitExample2 (master)
$ git push origin master
Enumerating objects: 4, done.
Counting objects: 100% (4/4), done.
Delta compression using up to 2 threads
Compressing objects: 100% (3/3), done.
Writing objects: 100% (3/3), 757.29 KiB | 6.95 MiB/s, done.
Total 3 (delta 1), reused 0 (delta 0)
remote: Resolving deltas: 100% (1/1), completed with 1 local object.
To https://github.com/ImDwivedi1/GitExample2.git
   828b962..0d5191f  master -> master
```

The file abc.jpg is successfully pushed to the origin master. We can track it on the remote location. I have pushed these changes to my GitHub account. I can track it there in my repository. Consider the below image:

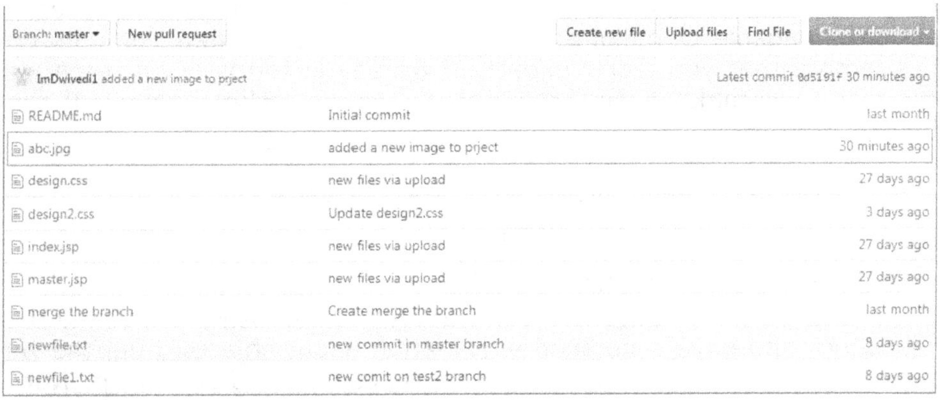

In the above output, the pushed file abc.jpg is uploaded on my GitHub account's master branch repository.

Git Force Push

The git force push allows you to push local repository to remote without dealing with conflicts. It is used as follows:

```
$ git push <remote><branch> -f
```

Or

```
$ git push <remote><branch> -force
```

The -f version is used as an abbreviation of force. The remote can be any remote location like GitHub, Subversion, or any other git service, and the branch is a particular branch name. For example, we can use git push origin master -f.

We can also omit the branch in this command. The command will be executed as:

```
$git push <remote> -f
```

We can omit both the remote and branch. When the remote and the branch both are omitted, the default behavior is determined by push.default setting of git config. The command will be executed as:

```
$ git push -f
```

How to Safe Force Push Repository:

There are several consequences of force pushing a repository like it may replace the work you want to keep. Force pushing with a lease option is capable of making fail to push if there are new commits on the remote that you didn't expect. If we say in terms of git, then we can say it will make it fail if remote contains untracked commit. It can be executed as:

```
$git push <remote><branch> --force-with-lease
```

Git push -v/--verbose

The -v stands for verbosely. It runs command verbosely. It pushed the repository and gave a detailed explanation about objects. Suppose we have added a newfile2.txt in our local repository and commit it. Now, when we push it on remote, it will give more description than the default git push. Syntax of push verbosely is given below:

Syntax:

```
$ git push -v
```

Or

```
$ git push --verbose
```

Consider the following output:

```
HiMaNshU@HiMaNshU-PC MINGW64 ~/Desktop/GitExample2 (master)
$ git push -v
Pushing to https://github.com/ImDwivedi1/GitExample2.git
Enumerating objects: 4, done.
Counting objects: 100% (4/4), done.
Delta compression using up to 2 threads
Compressing objects: 100% (2/2), done.
Writing objects: 100% (3/3), 289 bytes | 48.00 KiB/s, done.
Total 3 (delta 1), reused 0 (delta 0)
POST git-receive-pack (452 bytes)
remote: Resolving deltas: 100% (1/1), completed with 1 local object.
To https://github.com/ImDwivedi1/GitExample2.git
   0d5191f..56afce0  master -> master
updating local tracking ref 'refs/remotes/origin/master'
```

If we compare the above output with the default git option, we can see that git verbose gives descriptive output.

Delete a Remote Branch

We can delete a remote branch using git push. It allows removing a remote branch from the command line. To delete a remote branch, perform below command:

Syntax:

```
$ git push origin -delete edited
```

Output:

```
HiMaNshU@HiMaNshU-PC MINGW64 ~/Desktop/GitExample2 (master)
$ git push origin --delete edited
To https://github.com/ImDwivedi1/GitExample2.git
 - [deleted]         edited

HiMaNshU@HiMaNshU-PC MINGW64 ~/Desktop/GitExample2 (master)
$
```

In the above output, the git push origin command is used with -delete option to delete a remote branch. I have deleted my remote branch edited from the repository. Consider the following image:

It is a list of active branches of my remote repository before the operating command.

The above image displays the list of active branches after deleting command. Here, you can see that the branch edited has removed from the repository.

GIT Interview Questions

1) What is GIT?

Git is an open source distributed version control system and source code management (SCM) system with an insistence to control small and large projects with speed and efficiency.

2) Which language is used in Git?

Git uses 'C' language. Git is quick, and 'C' language makes this possible by decreasing the overhead of run times contained with high-level languages.

3) What is a repository in Git?

A repository consists of a list named .git, where git holds all of its metadata for the catalog. The content of the .git file is private to Git.

4) What is 'bare repository' in Git?

A "bare" repository in Git includes the version control information and no working files (no tree), and it doesn?t include the special. git sub-directory. Instead, it consists of all the contents of the .git sub-directory directly in the main directory itself, whereas working list comprises of:

A .git subdirectory with all the Git associated revision history of your repo.

A working tree, or find out copies of your project files.

5) What is the purpose of GIT stash?

GIT stash takes the present state of the working file and index and puts in on the stack for next and gives you back a clean working file. So in case if you are in the middle of object and require to jump over to the other task, and at the same time you don't want to lose your current edits, you can use GIT stash.

6) What is GIT stash drop?

When you are done with the stashed element or want to delete it from the directory, run the git 'stash drop' command. It will delete the last added stash item by default, and it can also remove a specific topic if you include as an argument.

7) What are the advantages of using GIT?

Here are some of the essential advantages of Git:

- ❖ Data repetition and data replication is possible
- ❖ It is a much applicable service
- ❖ For one depository you can have only one directory of Git
- ❖ The network performance and disk application are excellent
- ❖ It is effortless to collaborate on any project
- ❖ You can work on any plan within the Git
- ❖

8) What is the function of 'GIT PUSH' in GIT?

'GIT PUSH' updates remote refs along with related objects

9) Why do we require branching in GIT?

With the help of branching, you can keep your branch, and you can also jump between the different branches. You can go to your past work while at the same time keeping your recent work intact.

10) What is the purpose of 'git config'?

The 'Git config' is a great method to configure your choice for the Git installation. Using this command, you can describe the repository behavior, preferences, and user information.

11) What is the definition of "Index" or "Staging Area" in GIT?

When you are making the commits, you can make innovation to it, format it and review it in the common area known as 'Staging Area' or 'Index'.

12) What is a 'conflict' in git?

A 'conflict' appears when the commit that has to be combined has some change in one place, and the current act also has a change at the same place. Git will not be easy to predict which change should take precedence.

13) What is the difference between git pull and git fetch?

Git pull command pulls innovation or commits from a specific branch from your central repository and updates your object branch in your local repository.

Git fetch is also used for the same objective, but it works in a slightly different method. When you behave a git fetch, it pulls all new commits from the desired branch and saves it in a new branch in your local repository. If you need to reflect these changes in your target branch, git fetch should be followed with a git merge. Your target branch will only be restored after combining the target branch and fetched branch. To make it simple for you, remember the equation below:

Git pull = git fetch + git merge

14) How to resolve a conflict in Git?

If you need to resolve a conflict in Git, edit the list for fixing the different changes, and then you can run "git add" to add the resolved directory, and after that, you can run the 'git commit' for committing the repaired merge.

15) What is the purpose of the git clone?

The git clone command generates a copy of a current Git repository. To get the copy of a central repository, 'cloning' is the simplest way used by programmers.

16) What is git pull origin?

pull is a get and a consolidation. 'git pull origin master' brings submits from the master branch of the source remote (into the local origin/master branch), and then it combines origin/master into the branch you currently have looked out.

17) What does git commit a?

Git commits "records changes to the storehouse" while git push " updates remote refs along with contained objects" So the first one is used in a network with your local repository, while the latter one is used to communicate with a remote repository.

18) Why GIT better than Subversion?

GIT is an open source version control framework; it will enable you to run 'adaptations' of a task, which demonstrate the changes that were made to the code over time also it allows you keep the backtrack if vital and fix those changes. Multiple developers can check out, and transfer changes, and each change can then be attributed to a particular developer.

19) Explain what is commit message?

Commit message is a component of git which shows up when you submit a change. Git gives you a content tool where you can enter the adjustments made to a commit.

---

20) Why is it desirable to create an additional commit rather than amending an existing commit?

There are couples of reason

The correct activity will devastate the express that was recently saved in a commit. If only the commit message gets changed, that's not a problem. But if the contents are being modified, chances of excluding something important remains more.

Abusing "git commit- amends" can cause a small commit to increase and acquire inappropriate changes.

---

21) What does 'hooks' comprise of in Git?

This index comprises of Shell contents which are enacted after running the relating git commands. For instance, Git will attempt to execute the post-commit content after you run a commit.

---

22) What is the distinction between Git and Github?

A) Git is a correction control framework, a tool to deal with your source code history.

GitHub is a hosting function for Git storehouses.

GitHub is a website where you can transfer a duplicate of your Git archive. It is a Git repository hosting service, which offers the majority of the distributed update control and source code management (SCM) usefulness of Git just as including its features.

23) In Git, how would you return a commit that has just been pushed and made open?

There can be two answers to this question and ensure that you incorporate both because any of the below choices can be utilized relying upon the circumstance:

Remove or fix the bad document in another commit and push it to the remote repository. This is a unique approach to correct a mistake. Once you have necessary changes to the record, commit it to the remote repository for that I will utilize

git submit - m "commit message."

Make another commit that fixes all changes that were made in the terrible commit. to do this, I will utilize a command

git revert <name of bad commit>

24) What does the committed item contain?

Commit item contains the following parts; you should specify all the three present below:

A set of records, representing to the condition of a task at a given purpose of time

References to parent commit objects

An SHAI name, a 40 character string that uniquely distinguishes the commit object.

25) Describing branching systems you have utilized?

This question is a challenge to test your branching knowledge with Git along these lines, inform them regarding how you have utilized branching in your past activity and what reason does it serves, you can refer the below mention points:

Feature Branching:

A component branch model keeps the majority of the changes for a specific element within a branch. At the point when the item is throughout tested and approved by automated tests, the branch is then converged into master.

Task Branching

In this model, each assignment is actualized on its branch with the undertaking key included in the branch name. It is anything but difficult to see which code actualizes which task, search for the task key in the branch name.

Release Branching

Once the create branch has procured enough features for a discharge, you can clone that branch to frame a Release branch. Making this branch begins the following discharge cycle so that no new features can be included after this point, just bug fixes, documentation age, and other release oriented assignments ought to go in this branch. When it is prepared to deliver, the release gets converged into master and labeled with a form number. Likewise, it should be converged once again into creating a branch, which may have advanced since the release was started.

At last, disclose to them that branching methodologies fluctuate starting with one association then onto the next, so I realize essential branching activities like delete, merge, checking out a branch, etc.

---

26) By what method will you know in Git if a branch has just been combined into master?

The appropriate response is immediate.

To know whether a branch has been merged into master or not you can utilize the below commands:

git branch - merged It records the branches that have been merged into the present branch.

git brancha - no merged It records the branches that have not been merged.

27) How might you fix a messed up submit?

To fix any messed up commit, you will utilize the order "git commit?correct." By running this direction, you can set the wrecked commit message in the editor.

28) Mention the various Git repository hosting functions.

The following are the Git repository hosting functions:

- ❖ Pikacode
- ❖ Visual Studio Online
- ❖ GitHub
- ❖ GitEnterprise
- ❖ SourceForge.net

29) Mention some of the best graphical GIT customers for LINUX?

Some of the best GIT customer for LINUX is

- ❖ Git Cola
- ❖ Smart git
- ❖ Git-g
- ❖ Git GUI
- ❖ Giggle
- ❖ qGit

30) What is Subgit? Why use it?

'Subgit' is a tool that migrates SVN to Git. It is a stable and stress-free migration. Subgit is one of the solutions for a company-wide migration from SVN to Git that is:

- ❖ It is much superior to git-svn
- ❖ No need to change the infrastructure that is already placed.

- ❖ It allows using all git and all sub-version features.
- ❖ It provides stress ?free migration experience.

www.ingramcontent.com/pod-product-compliance
Lightning Source LLC
Chambersburg PA
CBHW052140070326
40690CB00047B/1328